"Gwen Farrell became a MUFON Field Investigator in 2006. In all the cases she handled, she displayed skill in gathering facts and data relevant to the reported event, while demonstrating an open-mindedness and willingness to consider alternative explanations. Her interactions with each reporting witness were always handled with compassion, concern and educated objectivity. Gwen is a trusted and valued member of our investigative team."

Stacey Wright
Asst. State Director
Arizona MUFON

FORBIDDEN QUESTIONS

A Guide to Human-ET Contact

Gwen Farrell, CHt, RT

Forbidden Questions: A Guide to Human-ET Contact
By Gwen Farrell, CHt, RT

Published in the United States by Lotus Dance Press, LLC
www.lotusdancepress.com

Cover Design and Interior Layout by Leslee Hare. www.lesleehare.net.
Set in Cambria.
Printed on acid-free paper supplied by a Forest Stewardship Council-certified provider, with chlorine-free ink.

Lotus Dance Press and the Dancing Figure colophon are registered trademarks of Lotus Dance Press, LLC. www.lotusdancepress.com

Dedication

It has been the greatest joy and privilege of my life to be part of what I call, for want of a better term, the UFO/ET phenomenon. This book is dedicated to all the brave and very special beings, wherever they are from, who have shared their amazing stories with me as a therapist, friend and fellow traveler.

I look forward to the day when there will be no more forbidden questions.

Acknowledgements

Thank you to my unfailingly dedicated and compassionate teachers and mentors, Barbara Lamb, the late Ruth Hover and Dolores Cannon, and the colleagues and friends with whom I am privileged to share my mission in this world and so much fun!

"Never, never make the mistake of thinking you're the only alien on the planet."

Kristin D. Randle

CONTENTS

CONTENTS

CONTENTS

Foreword by Barbara Lamb

The awareness of UFOs and people's encounters with extraterrestrial beings is increasing worldwide each year. Many people are aware that they have been having encounters with these beings and have been having them since very early childhood. Many other people are wondering if they have been having ET encounters because they are aware of having had clues, such as missing time, seeing bright light coming into their bedrooms at night, sensing and seeing unusual beings in their rooms at night, finding unusual markings on various parts of their bodies, feeling and seeing small lumps implanted under their skin, being followed by a beam of light while driving their car and having the car slowly come to a stop with the motor turned off, and some additional clues. These people may have wondered for decades about these unusual things that have happened to them. Very often they have not found anyone to disclose these happenings to and have lived with confusion and distress, with the memories held closely inside, unresolved.

For such people, it is a significant relief to find someone to talk to who knows about these unusual happenings and accepts them as very likely true, especially when that person takes them seriously and respectfully. It is even more gratifying to find such a person who additionally has the training, skill and ability to effectively conduct hypnotic regressions and counseling in order to find out the details and veracity of the suspected experiences. This brings significant relief to the person and answers a lot of questions and opens up new areas of understanding. This is help which the experiencer values tremendously.

Because the ETs have a way of successfully blocking a person's conscious awareness of an encounter, most people having ET encounters remember only the first few moments or the last few moments after they have been returned. Fortunately, the subconscious part of the person's mind has recorded the entire encounter, and in a hypnotic regression it can yield all the details of that encounter. A regression can give the person the sense of going back in time and reliving the event, from the first moment of awareness that something unusual is happening to the last moment of the event after being returned. The more the details of the material are realized by the person being regressed, the more the person can integrate what happened, find ways of coping with what has happened and gain a new sense of himself and of reality.

This is very meaningful work for people who have experienced ET encounters. It is also a significant contribution to the field of Ufology and to society at large. The ET beings who visit humans are very aware of us and want to learn as much about us as possible. It is important for us to learn about them and about the varying intents and agendas different groups of them have. Some of them seem to be more self-serving, yet others seem to be much more benevolent, caring and helpful to the people they interact with. We are all sharing this universe and it behooves us to be aware of and accepting of those other intelligent forms of life. As some of the ET-human hybrids living on Earth have told me "We are all ONE, we are not separate from each other, we are all part of The Creative Source."

It is extremely important that we not only have interest in the physical UFOs which we see in our skies and their technologies and propulsion systems, but that we get to know as much as possible about the beings who travel in those craft and intermingle with our people. Regressions to people's encounters with ETs often provide knowing more about these beings and their agendas, including the benevolent, helpful, spiritually inspiring aspect they enact.

The author of this book, Gwen Farrell, is abundantly qualified to address these issues and to help experiencers understand about what has happened to them in encounters with ET beings. She has conducted regressions with a significant number of experiencers and has conducted support groups for them as well. She has done considerable research about this phenomenon and has contributed valuable insights and perspective through her writings. This book brings fresh, new information about the phenomenon and is well worth adding to what you know about ET-Human relations.

Barbara Lamb, MS, MFT, CHT

Introduction

It has been estimated that thousands of people who are alive today have had contact with beings from other worlds. As a therapist who has worked with many of these people, I can unequivocally say that no one comes away from contact with alien beings unchanged or without questions; questions they are seldom able to answer on their own, and unhappily, when they reach out for help, they often encounter ridicule and condemnation rather than answers. After millennia of myth and legend, decades of formal investigation and nearly incontrovertible evidence that alien beings have visited Earth, humanity largely remains close-minded to that evidence, and contactees and researchers are still forbidden by society, science and religion from openly questioning and discussing this most important part of Earth history. These are the forbidden questions about human-ET contact.

In 2007, I began writing an internet blog as a global outreach to answer these questions and disseminate information about the various aspects of human-ET contact and disclosure that many people inside and outside the UFO/ET community were curious about and needed help with but couldn't talk about openly. As interest in the subject grew and more and more people found the blog to be an open, honest resource, some of the posts became articles that found their way into various professional journals and websites. Over the years, what my readers seemed to appreciate most about the blog, in addition to the subject matter, were its candor, impartiality and humor. This book represents the evolution of that blog, and although it's a bit longer and more formal than its predecessor, my goal is the same - to share what I know about human-ET contact honestly and simply, with a modicum of humor still lurking somewhere within.

Much has been written presenting different perspectives, theories and claims about the human-ET contact phenomenon. This book is not meant to refute them or debate them. Neither is it an encyclopedia, a research compendium, or a scientific treatise addressing the UFO/ET phenomenon from the perspective of technology, conspiracy theories, or politics. Instead, it's meant to add another voice to the discussion from the perspective of the human beings who know and live ET contact every day, for without the human perspective, there would be no UFO/ET phenomena.

Other Types of Experiences

Some experiencers report contact not only with extraterrestrial beings, but also anomalous events involving ghosts, angels, ascended beings and other paranormal entities, and some receive messages and downloads of information from beings who they believe exist in other realms or dimensions. Those types of incidents don't typically manifest the same way ET abduction and contacts events do, but regardless of whether the contact is with ETs or other beings, the common denominator appears to be the human mind, spirit and consciousness. While I have some experience in the area of paranormal happenings, they aren't my specialty, so I do not address the subject fully in this book. However, I have included the names and contact information of some individuals who are experts on the subject in the Resources section of this book.

The Truth, the Whole Truth and Nothing but the Truth

People sometimes ask me if I believe all the stories experiencers tell me about their supposed contact with aliens, and how do I know they're not just making it all up? Well, I've been doing this work long enough to have a pretty good idea about the veracity of the stories I hear, but as a therapist, it's really not my job to determine that. My job is to be there if someone asks for help, to listen and do what I can to assist them in their search for answers and healing. Everyone's truth is their own and no one, not even their therapist, can find it for them. Sometimes it's relatively easy, sometimes it's very hard, but after the many years I've done this work, I am still amazed at the power and resilience of the human mind and spirit to heal and move forward. When it comes to the human-ET phenomenon, I admit that I don't know the whole truth, and I don't think anyone else does either, but hopefully, we are all moving toward that knowledge.

What I Know

As a therapist, my goal is to help individuals progress from issues to solutions one step at a time along their own path, be it short and straight or long and winding. My therapy experience and years of study and work in the UFO/ET field forms the foundation of this book. Of course, I have my own opinions and beliefs, but a good therapist doesn't tell her clients what to believe or what to do; instead, she strives to help them see their issues, options and goals clearly, then find a way forward that works for them. It has always been my intention as a therapist, and in writing this book, to present information that can help readers find their own true answers.

In my roles as a UFO investigator, therapist, and consciousness researcher, I have seen all aspects of the UFO/ET phenomenon, and I believe that gives me a perspective on the subject that not many others in the field are privileged to have. At the same time, I don't claim to know everything there is to know about human-ET contact, nor do I claim to speak for everyone who has experienced it.

What I do know is that the hundreds of individuals who have told me their stories, have asked the questions and have faced ridicule, or worse, as a result, aren't making it all up. Something very important is happening to humanity, and it's my hope that my continued work will help hasten the day when there will be no forbidden questions.

Terminology

Certain terms are used interchangeably in this book, which may cause some confusion, especially to readers who aren't familiar with standard UFO/ET terminology, so before going further, I'll try to clarify.

The term "UFO" is an acronym for "unidentified flying object" and, technically, means any object in the sky that can't be identified. In popular jargon, however, the term usually refers to flying saucers or other alien craft. To distinguish between the two in this book, I use "unidentified flying object" when I refer to an object in the sky that can't be identified, and "UFO" when I refer to alien craft or possible alien craft. It may sound confusing, but it should make sense when read in context. "ET," "extraterrestrial," "alien," and "otherworldly beings" are used interchangeably; as are "abduction," "experience," "contact" and "contact event." "USO" is an acronym that stands for unidentified submerged object - any object or optical or mechanical detection phenomenon of unknown origin observed under water that remains unidentified even after thorough investigation. While these anomalous events aren't as common as UFOs, they do happen and have been reported throughout the world.

A new acronym introduced to the world by the FREE study is "NHI," which stands for non-human intelligence, a term that encompasses extraterrestrial, interdimensional and paranormal beings.

Final Notes

And last, but certainly not least, I want to make it clear that while I am a trained, qualified and certified hypnotherapist and experiencer therapist, I am not a psychologist, psychiatrist or medical professional. I have never claimed to be, nor have I ever exceeded my training or skill level while working as an experiencer therapist. Over the years, I have relied on the advice and guidance of medical professionals in my practice and have referred clients and non-client experiencers to medical professionals when I felt it was appropriate. I know very well the complexity of the human mind and personality and the effect that contact with alien beings can have on a person's life, and I would never jeopardize anyone's physical or mental health. Anything in this book referring to human anatomy, physiology, or psychology is included for informational purposes only and should not be considered the opinion of a medical professional.

Muchas Gracias!

I want to express my many thanks to the individuals who helped and supported me in this project and those who allowed me to include portions of their contact experiences, opinions and advice in this book. It wasn't easy for some of them to come forward, and I very much appreciate their trust in me. At their request, only their initials have been used and, except for minor editing for spelling and punctuation, the words are theirs.

Thank you all for your part in my journey!

"Not for ourselves alone are we born."

Marcus Tullius Cicero

Introduction to Second Edition

When the first copies of *Forbidden Questions: A Therapist Talks About Human-ET Contact* rolled off the press in November 2017, there were events in motion that I expected to come to fruition, but didn't know when, so I elected to go ahead and publish, knowing there would probably be a second edition within the next year or two. Now here it is!

The usual purpose of a second edition is to revise and update the original book as subsequent events occur or new information becomes available, all of which apply in this case. Since I began working on *Forbidden Questions* in 2017, the *New York Times* released a stunning announcement about a clandestine program run by the Pentagon to investigate potential extraterrestrial attacks, admitting, without a doubt, that the United States government has known about the presence, and possible threat status, of UFOs for years; the leader of a popular rock band launched a new organization comprised of experienced and connected members of the US intelligence community, including the CIA and Department of Defense, "to bring transformative science and engineering out of the shadows and collaborate with global citizens to apply that knowledge in a way that benefits humanity"; and the world's first comprehensive academic multilingual research study on contact between human and non-human intelligent beings was completed and published. If things keep moving at the same pace, by the time I get this second edition out, it'll be time for a third.

Regardless of how many editions there eventually prove to be, my overall goal will remain the same, to talk about human-ET contact directly and honestly from the human experiencer's point of view. When the ETs are ready, they will speak out for themselves. There may come a day when the big picture of UFOs and ETs on Earth is complete, but at this time it's my belief that no individual researcher or investigator has sufficient information to fill that in. However, the new material included in this edition will definitely add more pieces to the puzzle.

Surprising New Survey Results

In August 2018, The Dr. Edgar Mitchell Foundation for Research into Extraterrestrial and Extraordinary Experiences (FREE) published *Beyond UFOs: The Science of Consciousness and Contact with Non-Human*

Intelligence - Volume 1,[1] in which it presents and analyzes the results of a four-year survey of 3,970 individuals who reported having contact with alien beings (the "FREE Study"). The scientifically-conducted survey produced ground-breaking results in the area of human-ET contact. I am very pleased to have the permission of FREE to include their findings in my research and I have referred to them throughout this book.

Easy Answers to Difficult Questions

It's human nature to question the world around us and to want instant, easy answers. Easy answers may get us quickly from one point to another, stimulate our mental processes and sometimes lead us to deeper truths, but much of the time, they're not real answers - they're just easy. This applies to all areas of research and investigation, including the area of human-ET contact. A lot of people have answers which they are more than willing to disseminate as truth from the podiums of conferences and via books and the internet, and it's easy for the rest of us to listen, read and assume that because the information is coming from someone standing on a stage, it must be the truth, without considering that it might be just an easy answer.

We all want to know what's going on between otherworldly beings and humans on Earth, actually why they are here and what they want with us, and we want it spelled out in simple, clear, easy-to-understand answers, and if the ETs finally ever do decide to spell it out for us, then we will know. But in the meantime, I can't give you the answers and, in my opinion, neither can any investigator, researcher, scientist, or anyone else who is on the public stage at this point in time. If contact is all about consciousness, which it appears to be, then we are just beginning to understand how vast the big picture is. We must keep our minds open to all possibilities - not just the easy answers.

More Forbidden Questions

Unfortunately, the veil of secrecy and repression around the history and current presence and activities of extraterrestrials on Earth and the world governments' relations with them has not lifted since I

---

[1] The Dr. Edgar Mitchell Foundation for Research into Extraterrestrial and Extraordinary Experiences (FREE), *Beyond UFOs: The Science of Consciousness and Contact with Non Human Intelligence - Volume 1, 2019.*

published the first edition of this book in 2017. Important questions are still being asked and there are still no mainstream public forums to discuss the answers. Whether for good or not, this book contains more questions and more possible answers.

"I wonder if aliens deny that we exist?"

Anthony T. Hincks

THE

FORBIDDEN

QUESTIONS

1

Q: What is an experiencer?

Human contact with otherworldly beings is widely varied. For most people who go through them, such events prove to be the most frightening, enlightening and weighty happenings of their lives. Although the media and entertainment industry tend to pigeonhole contact with extraterrestrial beings into a limited range of images that fit neatly into news blurbs and movie story lines, in reality, it is far more than that.

According to firsthand accounts by individuals who have been there, it's possible to come face-to-face with alien beings in different places and at different times, and to find oneself entangled in a maze of inexplicable experiences, in daylight or at night, once in a lifetime or more. Some experiencers think they are going crazy, some think they are seeing angels, demons or ghosts, and some think it's just a dream and roll over and go back to sleep.

In the past, popular culture and Ufology has lumped all ET contact events into the general domain of "abductions" without attempting to characterize them further. However, contemporary comprehensive research and investigation of reported contacts reveal that such events are not homogeneous; indeed, they are quite varied in nature and effect. Based on current research and reporting, the terms "abduction" and "abductee" no longer accurately describe or represent the multi-faceted aspects of the contact experience, and thus, they have generally been replaced in the UFO/ET lexicon by the terms "experience," "experiencer" and "contactee," although the older terms are still used.

Dictionaries define the word "experiencer" simply as "someone who experiences something." The field of psychology defines an experiencer as "the thing that experiences the effect of an action, state or process" or "the thing, feeling or being affected by an experience." Based on those definitions, since we are all affected by different experiences every day, in truth, we are all experiencers. But in the context of this book and in the field of human-ET contact, the term "experiencer" means much more. Of course, not all human beings experience contact with UFOs and ETs, although I suspect many people have had such experiences, but either don't recall or want to admit them.

In the field of Ufology, an experiencer is an individual who has had contact with extraterrestrial or interdimensional beings, without regard to the circumstances, location or nature of the contact. Every year, thousands of people see lights in the sky they believe are flying saucers or other alien craft, but upon investigation, turn out to be animals, weather effects or conventional aircraft. Most of the time the lights pass by with no physical contact or trace left behind.

But in rare instances, the lights do prove to be something more, and contact happens.

"Some friends and I were camping at the lake and the sun had just gone down, not real dark yet though, when we saw this light moving across the sky really low from the north to the south. My girlfriend noticed it first and we all stopped to look as it moved toward us. It wasn't real big, just sorta oval and bright. We watched it until it got right over us and then it stopped, right above us. I don't know how long it was there but I guess it was just a few seconds. This is really weird, but I had the feeling that it was somehow familiar to me, like it knew me and like it was doing something to me but it was okay and I wasn't scared. Then the next thing I remember it took off straight up and we all started talking like crazy trying to figure out what it was. After that we headed into town to a bar and had a lot to drink and got back out to camp late and went to bed and headed home the next day and didn't say anything about it. About a week later my girlfriend told me she had been having dreams about the light and she described that she felt just like I had, that it was familiar to her, and she said it had given her information and told her that she wouldn't understand it then but she would later. The next time we all got together, we started talking about it, and it turns out all of us who had been at the lake and seen the light or UFO or whatever it was were having the same kinds of dreams and feeling like they had been given some kind of information." TR

Q: What is an experiencer?

In the years that I have worked as an investigator and therapist, I have observed that incidents of physical experiences, such as abductions and transport to alien craft, are being reported less frequently, while incidents of psychic contact have increased. Many experiencers who began having physical abductions when they were children report their contact is now exclusively psychic. Interestingly, not only has the contact changed in form, the effects have changed as well. Not all abduction-type contact has disappeared, but there seems to be a trend in that direction. We don't know why, but it may be that the ETs who took human beings in the past are no longer working with humanity, or those who are working with us now aren't interested in the kind of information that requires our physical presence. Certainly, psychic contact is less traumatic and more efficient than transporting humans to and from ships or other locations.

For some experiencers, contact begins in childhood and ceases at puberty; for others, it runs continuously throughout their lives. Some individuals are visited frequently - every week or every month - and some only once or twice every few years. Some experiencers are alerted to upcoming contact by dreams, psychic messages or visual images. Some people experience feelings of anticipation or physical sensations, such as buzzing or ringing in their ears before contact, and some are taken completely by surprise, with no warning at all. After contact, some experiencers have memories of the event to which they respond with joy and feelings of privilege and blessing, even with eager anticipation of future contact; while others react with fear, dread and confusion, perhaps doubting their sanity. In most cases, there is no conscious memory or, at best, only vague partial recollections or recurring dreams that don't make sense.

The human-ET contact phenomenon is vast and complex, and individuals from all walks of life are interested in it. The explosion of science fiction in art, literature and all forms of entertainment is proof of that. In that context, human-ET contact stories are great fun, but in reality, interaction with alien beings is serious business that often leaves experiencers struggling with confusion, fear and haunting questions. Even positive interactions with alien beings can be overwhelming.

Contact with alien beings is not normal, and yet for the most part, experiencers are normal people with families, jobs and routine lives. At the same time, they are amazing individuals with the strength and grace to persevere through what are often the most frightening and remarkable ordeals human beings can experience - contact with extra-terrestrial beings.

"The Experiencer of contact with non-human intelligence is the 'key' that will open the door to understanding what is consciousness and what is the relationship between consciousness and contact with non-human intelligence."

Dr. Edgar Mitchell, FREE Co-Founder

2

Q: Am I an experiencer?

Many people have seen a UFO - an unidentified flying object - they thought might be of extraterrestrial origin at least once in their lives. Usually it passes by without incident and is never seen again. Or if investigated, turns out to be a conventional explainable object. Those are the types of sightings I mostly investigated when I was a UFO field investigator, because they made up the majority of reports submitted by everyday people in my part of the world. And although I no longer keep close track of UFO sighting statistics, I would bet they are still the most common. Even though I no longer wear my field investigator hat, not a month goes by that someone doesn't excitedly tell me about a light they saw in the sky the night before that they are sure was an alien craft. And who knows, maybe it was. We all want to believe we've seen a flying saucer, while the truth is, in most instances, we haven't.

But sometimes, we actually do find ourselves in up-close, face-to-face encounters with craft and occupants who are undeniably extraterrestrial. Such contact events may occur in out-of-the-way places in the dark of night or normal everyday environments during the day, and may involve individuals in a wide range of circumstances, individually or in groups. Some individuals may have conscious recall of these events and some may not. For some, encounters with otherworldly craft and beings are traumatic and destructive; for others, they are positive, uplifting and life-affirming. In addition to the vast number of individuals alive on Earth today who are convinced that they have had ET contact, it's estimated that there are millions more who are also experiencers, but who haven't realized it yet. Consequently, contact between ETs and human beings is probably much more common than generally thought.

If you think you might be an experiencer, how do you know for sure? Human-ET contact events are as unique as the individuals who live them, but similarities can be found among many. A few studies and surveys on the nature and effects of contact on human beings have been published to date and, while the following is not an exhaustive list, it represents the most commonly reported signs of ET contact. Of course, there are normal explanations for most of these as well, but the plausibility of contact increases when the signs can be connected to sightings of unidentified flying objects.

So keeping that in mind, if you have had all or most of the following experiences connected to the sighting of a UFO, it's likely that you are an experiencer.

Have you experienced missing time - a period of time that you can't account for?

In some cases of contact, experiencers recall driving somewhere when something strange and unexpected happened to them and they arrived at their destination safely, but later than planned, with no rational explanation. There may be minutes or hours they can't account for at the time, but within a few days, weeks or longer, they may remember, or they may have a dream in which they see their drive being interrupted by a craft that suddenly appeared above the road and non-human beings taking them into the craft and releasing them sometime later. This is just one type of missing time event; there are many others. Missing time has been reported in many different locales and circumstances, and while it isn't always involved, it is a common aspect of human-ET contact. If you have experienced a period of missing time in connection with the sighting of an unidentified flying object, it's likely that you are an experiencer.

After a suspected contact event, have you found marks on your body that defy rational explanation?

Experiencers sometimes report finding marks on their bodies, including circle or triangle-shaped marks, bruises, burns, etc., they think might be the result of contact with extraterrestrial beings. But there may be logical explanations for such marks, such as insect bites, injuries, allergic reactions and skin aging, that weren't noticed at the time they happened. Contact doesn't always result in physical marks, so the presence or absence of a mark without knowledge or suspicion of ET contact cannot be considered conclusive evidence. However, such marks are often found as the result of contact events and may mean that you are an experiencer.

If you find a suspicious mark on your body in connection with a UFO sighting and you want to document it, you should get some good photographs of the mark (a black light can sometimes make marks more visible), write a description of the mark and the location on your body, and the circumstances in which you think it happened, then have a doctor examine the mark to determine what it is. And, of course, if you are ill or injured, get medical help immediately.

Please Note: Possible evidence of ET physical contact on your body is very personal. Don't feel that you must share such information or evidence with anyone, including investigators or researchers, if you don't want to. As much as we all want irrefutable proof of contact, no one has the right to violate your privacy in pursuit of that proof.

Have you found a foreign object anywhere in your body that didn't get there by normal, explainable means?

Some experiencers report finding objects they believe were implanted in their bodies during contact with extraterrestrial beings. Implants are thought to be utilized for various purposes, but the most common may be for tracking human subjects' locations and biological status, and as healing devices. Although many objects thought to be alien implants have been removed from human bodies over the years, very few have been thoroughly studied and compared, so there is still a lack of solid evidence about their origins and purposes. Such devices are usually difficult to preserve, rapidly degrading once they are removed from the body. Like marks left by ET contact on the body, alien implants are not part of every contact scenario, but they are sometimes reported, and if you have one and you want it investigated, be sure to document it thoroughly. Also, like marks found on your body, you have the right to privacy regarding physical examination and removal.

Have you found wounds on your body or have you experienced unexpected bleeding from natural body openings or unexplainable pain in body cavities?

Some experiencers report that during experiments or procedures by alien beings, natural body openings were penetrated or probed by tools, instruments or energies that resulted in pain, bleeding, bruising or other tissue damage that could not be attributed to injury or disease pre-existing the ET contact. Implants may also sometimes be found in those locations. Of course, bleeding from the mouth, nose and other body openings may result from normal physical illness or other issues; however, if you experience such in connection with the sighting of an unidentified flying object and you can't attribute it to anything else, you may be an experiencer.

If you are female, have you unexpectedly become pregnant or experienced anything unusual relating to a pregnancy?

Many women report participating in alien procedures related to reproduction and recall being impregnated with alien or human-alien DNA or being implanted with alien fetuses as part of hybridization programs. Often, such implants end in miscarriages due to incompatibilities between human and alien physiology. Some female experiencers also report having their fetuses removed by the experimenting ETs before they reach full term. Even normal pregnancies are not always without problems and, in most cases, alien beings are not involved. But if you have experienced abnormalities in connection with pregnancies and have had recent sightings of UFOs, you may be an experiencer.

Have members of your family had contact experiences?

Research indicates that ET contact often runs in families, which may indicate that ETs are monitoring certain genetic lines for specific purposes. However, contact has also occurred in blended families where there was no genetic link, so at least in those situations, ETs seem to have familial interests that extend beyond blood line. Perhaps families who have ET contact are more accepting and less resistant to continuing contact. Some experiencers report seeing their brothers or sisters being taken along with them, but later when they are questioned about it, the siblings deny being taken. Perhaps they actually don't recall the event or they just don't want to talk about it. Not all members of a family may have had contact, but it's fairly common, so if someone in your family is an experiencer, it's likely that you are too.

Have you ever awakened with your clothing turned inside-out or backward, or found yourself wearing clothing that was not yours?

Reports of this type are rare, but not unheard of. Many experiencers say they see other humans aboard alien ships, they are usually naked and they are almost always in an altered state of consciousness, so it would be easy to get the wrong clothing. For this and other reasons, investigators always advise experiencers to retain and preserve whatever they were wearing before and after the contact event. If you have awakened wearing clothing that did not belong to you or someone else in your home, or with damage to your own clothing that you can't account for, it's likely that you are an experiencer.

Do you have frequent, vivid dreams about alien abduction or contact experiences?

When you are asleep and your conscious mind is taking a break, memories may emerge from your subconscious mind during dreaming. Such memories frequently have emotions attached to them that make them very vivid and powerful. If you are an experiencer and memories of contact events are still in your subconscious mind, they may come out in vivid dreams or nightmares about the events.

Have you seen beings that didn't look human in your bedroom or elsewhere, including public places?

While most reported abduction events begin at night in an individual's bedroom or another room in their home, contact events do occur in other locations, even in public places. Some ETs may appear and behave enough like humans that they can live and work among us undetected, and they may be attempting to assume human identities and assimilate into society for a variety of reasons. However, individuals who are especially sensitive or have heightened ESP or intuitive abilities may be able to identify human-appearing ETs. If you can see these alien beings, it may be because you possess advanced psychic abilities or you may be an experiencer.

Do you have memories of being inside an extraterrestrial craft and interacting with the occupants?

Not all human-ET contact events take place aboard alien craft, but many experiencers do relate being taken from their homes or other Earth environments and transported to ships where they interact with ETs and sometimes other humans. If you have memories of this happening to you, you may be an experiencer.

Do you have trouble falling asleep and sleeping through the night for unexplained reasons?

Traumatic events of any type can cause disruption of sleep, and there are many reasons why you might have trouble falling asleep and staying asleep throughout the night. But experiencers may find it especially difficult or impossible to fall asleep and remain asleep due to nightmares, memories of past contact or fear of future contact. If you have trouble sleeping, you have investigated and ruled out all the normal causes, and you have had sightings of what you believe were UFOs, you may be an experiencer.

Do you feel fear or anxiety over the subject of UFOs or ETs?

If you feel nervous or uncomfortable around anything pertaining to UFOs or ETs, you could be experiencing fear caused by a past contact event, even one you don't remember. Much of what is presented in the media, movies, video games, etc., about aliens is frightening and repulsive enough to cause even non-experiencers to cringe, but if contact has happened or is happening to you, exposure to similar material can be even more unnerving. If taken to the extreme, it may even manifest in a phobia that can have serious and long-term effects. If you feel unusually fearful when you see TV shows, movies or pictures of UFOs or ETs, you may be an experiencer.

Do you have a deep conviction that you are on Earth for a special purpose or mission, but you may not know what it is?

It's not uncommon for people to have strong interests in certain things in their lives that can be attributed to normal genetic, societal and environmental influences. But individuals who have contact with extraterrestrial beings often have an especially strong sense that they are part of something beyond their physical, earthly existence. This conviction may motivate and shape them throughout their lives, and yet they may not truly understand its presence or purpose until their true stories are revealed to them. If you have a deep personal conviction that you may be on Earth for a special purpose that you don't understand, you may be an experiencer.

A more extensive list of possible signs of ET contact can be found in the Appendix section of this book.

So what should you do?

If you believe you are an experiencer and you are okay with that, you don't really need to do anything. But if you are interested in looking into the possibility, one-on-one experiencer therapy may be helpful, or support groups and meet-ups can help fill in the gaps, answer questions and encourage your own recollections. Keep in mind, though, that there are a lot of differing opinions and beliefs about UFOs, ETs and contact, not all of which are helpful, so don't get involved in a group that you don't feel good about. If the possibility that you are an experiencer is creating difficulties in your life, you should talk to a qualified therapist or counselor who is also knowledgeable in the UFO/ET field. If you find that you are an experiencer, for good or ill, your life will never be the same.

Human-ET contact is amazing and complicated. Some people who are not experiencers wish they were, and some people who are experiencers wish they were not. If you are an experiencer, I hope it's a positive and enlightening adventure for you. But if it isn't, I hope you'll reach out for help dealing with the difficulties, and remember that you're not alone. There are people who can help, if that's what you want.

"We may not remember it clearly. We may think it is only a dream. We may ignore the signs of extraterrestrial contact simply because we do not understand them. And most of all, we may simply be too frightened to acknowledge its presence. When we as a species evolve, so will the nature of our contact experiences."

Lyssa Royal-Holt

3

Q: Should I get therapy for my ET contact experiences?

Not necessarily. While all human-ET contact events share similarities, each experience is as individual as the person who experiences it. Human-ET contact can manifest in a multitude of ways and can happen only once or over and over throughout the course of a lifetime. Some experiencers respond to these occurrences with joy and a feeling of blessing and privilege, even eagerly anticipating the next occurrence; while many others react with fear and frustration, maybe even doubting their sanity. Most individuals have only vague partial recollections of their contact experiences or dreams they don't understand that fill them with confusion and dread. They may realize they need help, but not know where to turn or who to turn to. If they are then faced with skepticism or ridicule from their peers or the condemnation of family, friends or religious authorities, their situation can become even more difficult and their search for help more desperate. Therapy can be very helpful in working through issues that arise from contact, but it may not always be necessary.

Occasionally, memories of contact events return on their own over a period of time, but when they do, they are frequently too confusing and frightening for an individual to deal with alone. At that point, many experiencers realize the value of consulting a therapist who has the tools to help them sift through emerging memories and gain an understanding and clear perspective on them.

Therapy

Serious medical or psychological issues resulting from contact with extraterrestrial beings should always be referred to medical or mental health professionals. But for experiencers who are not suffering that level of trauma, Experiencer Therapy may be effective. Depending on their experience and training, the therapist may utilize a variety of counseling and therapeutic techniques, including hypnotherapy, depending on what is needed for a particular individual. However, it's not the only tool available to help experiencers.

For the last one hundred years, hypnosis has proved safe and beneficial in a variety of applications, including mental and behavioral issues, childbirth, preparation for and recovery from surgery, pain control and the palliative care of cancer patients to reduce the symptoms associated with radiation and chemotherapy, in addition to experiencer therapy. But there is still confusion and misunderstanding about it.

We all go in and out of natural hypnotic states of mind all the time. Common examples are daydreaming or losing track of time while you're deeply focused on a work project, reading a book or watching a movie, or driving somewhere and suddenly realizing that you have arrived, but not recalling the details of the drive. A hypnotherapy session is similar, but with a structure and a specific purpose.

Are there problems with hypnosis?

Like all therapeutic techniques, hypnosis is limited to what it can accomplish. While it has proven effective in recovering memories of ET contact and working through issues that may arise as a result of contact, it doesn't work for everyone. And the argument that hypnosis can encourage the creation of fantasies and inaccurate memories is not completely false. It can happen, which is why it's important to consult a qualified, experienced therapist who knows what they're doing.

Some people are concerned that if they undergo hypnosis to recall a contact event, they will somehow be placing themselves under the control of the therapist or will end up brainwashed. That is not true. The fact is that under hypnosis alone, it's impossible for an individual to be coerced into doing anything that is not ethically acceptable to them, such as committing a crime or harming themselves or someone else. Brainwashing requires a tremendous amount of specialized skill, time and effort to accomplish - separating the subject from their daily environment and subjecting them to abnormal, continuous psychological pressure, physical torture, deprivation and often the use of powerful drugs. Thankfully, hypnosis alone is simply not strong enough to brainwash someone.

Therapists

Most experiencer therapists are licensed and/or certified professionals trained in various counseling and therapeutic techniques, who use hypnosis in a therapeutic manner. A hypnotherapist should, at the very least, be certified in basic hypnosis and therapeutic techniques with additional training in psychology and counseling. An experiencer therapist who intends to utilize hypnosis should be a certified hypno-therapist and, additionally, be knowledgeable in the UFO/ET phenom-enon. If they have experience in investigations and research, that's a plus. Even if someone is a medical professional, he or she should be knowledgeable in the UFO/ET field. Experiencers have the right to ex-pect that their therapist is a qualified and experienced professional with a thorough understanding of the contact phenomenon as well.

Experiencer therapy can consist of a few sessions of therapy and counseling or up to several weeks or months, with support group fol-low-up, depending on the individual's needs. When it comes to effective therapy, there is no ONE-SIZE-FITS-ALL. Many therapists offer a free consultation to explain the type of therapy they do and determine if they can help you. But keep in mind that everyone is different and it's impossible to say up front exactly how long it will take to get you where you want to be.

If it ain't broke, don't fix it

Many people ask me if they should get therapy to recover memo-ries of their ET contact experiences or help them deal with the experi-ences they already remember, and I always ask this question in return, "Are your experiences causing problems for you?" If the answer is No, I tell them they probably don't need therapy. On the other hand, if the answer is Yes, I suggest that they speak with a therapist or counselor and consider therapy. Some individuals who don't have problems with their contact experiences, but who want to explore them further, may also find therapy helpful.

What it boils down to is this: just because someone is an experi-encer, doesn't mean they need therapy.

Pros and cons

Experiencer therapy and counseling have been shown to help lessen chronic anxiety caused by dreams and intrusive thoughts that often follow ET experiences, and enable an individual to gain new in-sight into years of possible misunderstood or unexplained behavior rooted in those experiences. Troublesome issues such as phobias and obsessive-compulsive behaviors that may stem from ET contact often decrease or disappear completely when such experiences are carefully and competently explored and reconciled. Many experiencers report that after working through their disturbing contact memories, confusion and fear in therapy, they are finally able to get on with their lives with newly found confidence in themselves and their abilities to deal with adversity. Coming to terms with any issue is the first step to overcoming it, and therapy can bring abduction/contact memories into normal recall, where an experiencer can ultimately come terms with them. Research has shown that people who have chosen to work with a qualified counselor or experiencer therapist to explore their ET experiences are almost always satisfied with the decision.

If you are an experiencer, or think you may be, and if you're considering therapy, you should look carefully at a few facts before going ahead with it.

1. Know that your decision to explore your possible ET contact experiences will be one of the most important decisions you ever make. If you discover that you are an experiencer and come to understand the ramifications, there will be no turning back. Your life will never be the same. It may be positive or negative, but whichever it is, it will be a turning point in your life. Are you ready for that?

2. An important consideration is timing. Are there things going on in your life - family or work problems, health issues, etc. - that might make you more vulnerable at a particular time? Exploration of abduction/contact memories can be traumatic and take a long time to work through, and problems or instability in your work or personal life may not provide a secure foundation for what comes up. So it might be better to wait until a more stable period in your life before proceeding.

3. Hypnosis is a natural function of the mind that we all experience every day, but when it comes to hypnosis with specific goals, most people need more than one session to see significant results. Of course, everyone is different, but keep in mind that an exploration of your contact experiences may be time-consuming and costly. This type of work cannot be rushed. Will your budget of time and money permit such expenditures?

4. Keep in mind that memories often do not reflect reality, and always strive to retain a healthy skepticism of them. The human mind is very complex and memories are notoriously undependable. People

sometimes remember events incorrectly, create imaginary scenarios (consciously or unconsciously) and remember things that didn't happen or that happened differently, and the more traumatic the experience, the more undependable the memories are likely to be. This is especially true with memories of abduction/contact events. Further muddling things, some experiencers report that ETs are adept at mental manipulation, causing a person to see things that are not there or to see things differently from what they actually are. It's important to seek the help of a competent, experienced therapist who can help you recover valid memories and assist you in navigating through them.

5. There are no guarantees. As effective as hypnosis and therapy can be, they are not appropriate for everyone. As I said before, the human mind is very complex, with lots of twists and turns that sometimes cannot be charted to our satisfaction, and if your mind doesn't want to share its secrets, there is nothing an ethical therapist or counselor can do to make that happen. A therapist cannot make you remember anything, and you will not be able to remember anything on your own that your mind is not ready to give up. That said, if you and your mind are open, much can be accomplished.

6. Freshly recalled abduction/contact events can cause unexpected revelations and bring up other issues. Such revelations can alter relationships with family and friends, who might not be able to handle the implications that arise or who may doubt your veracity or sanity. While some experiencers have patient, compassionate back-up systems, sadly, they are in the minority. Are you prepared for the possibility of having to make this journey without the support of your family and friends?

7. If you are comfortable sharing your experiences with other people and are willing to listen to theirs, you might benefit from an experiencer support group rather than private therapy. A group can be a good place to start and may be all you need, and you can meet people you share a lot with and who won't think you're nuts - at least no more than they are.

There are a variety of support group types that may be helpful and enjoyable.

- *Therapist-facilitated groups* are led by a therapist or counselor, they may be open or by referral, and meetings may or may not include therapy as a regular component.

- *Peer-facilitated groups*, meet-ups or UFO and paranormal interest groups are usually informal get-togethers that advertise on-line or in local magazines or newspapers and don't include therapy.

- *Experiencer groups at conferences* are informal meetings facilitated by qualified therapists or counselors who may also be conference speakers. They are usually offered at least once a day and may or may not charge admission.

Experiencer groups can be helpful in recalling and working through abduction/contact experiences on a lighter level and are less expensive than private therapy. They can help you develop friendships and feel less isolated. However, they may not be as effective as private therapy, you won't get the individual guidance and personal support you may need, and you'll need to exercise judgment about the group's motives and intentions. In addition, support groups should be temporary and supportive, and not be relied on as mechanisms to enable or mask issues that result from contact experiences.

Self therapy

As mentioned elsewhere in this book, memories of abduction/contact events can return on their own, gradually over time or in chunks or floods if they receive the correct stimulus, and often it doesn't need to be much more than a sight, sound or even a fragrance. The problem with that type of remembering, though, is that it is often haphazard and frightening, and may not make sense. One avenue of help at that point can be therapy or counseling, as I've discussed, but it may also be possible to recall experiences - ET and non-ET - through certain kinds of meditation or self-hypnosis techniques.

While meditation is a wonderful way to relax and de-stress, it is also a very powerful way of harnessing the power of the mind to acquire new knowledge and skills. The phrase "mind over matter" is not a joke. Not only can the mind be used to acquire knowledge from outside itself, it can also reach inward for hidden, misplaced or forgotten information such as memories.

Meditation to recall a contact event can be as simple as finding a quiet, comfortable place to be alone; relaxing, make an intention that you will recall whatever you want to recall, safely and without trauma; going over what you do remember of the event; and letting your mind do the rest. It may take several attempts to achieve anything, and it might not work at all, because there are no guarantees. But if nothing comes back to you during the meditation session, you may find that things begin to come back to you later, or things you knew before but didn't understand, may now begin to make sense. Memories are not dangerous and they can't hurt you, but they may have emotions attached to them that are difficult to deal with, and in that case you may find it best to seek help from a therapist or counselor rather than going it alone.

Self-hypnosis may also be helpful for recovering your contact memories on your own. Like meditation, there are many variations on basic techniques that are available and can be very effective.

Journaling

Whether you decide to work with a therapist, in a group or on your own, keeping a journal of what you remember about your contact events may be a good idea. Not only can it help clarify memories of recent events, it can also serve as a basis for other memories that you may recall in the future and prevent details from being lost over time. If you are diligent about writing down details as you remember them - even small bits and pieces - after a while, things can begin to come together and form a complete picture. If you want to journal:

- You can either write, type or record your journal entries, whichever you prefer, but it's imperative that you do so as soon as possible after the contact happens. The longer you wait, the less you'll remember.

- Include as many descriptions of what happened as you can remember, including smells, sounds and emotions.

- Accuracy is not as important as making a record of the information. Just write down or record as much as you can remember at the time.

- Try not to make judgments at the time, just record as much as you can remember, then take a look at your journal after a few months.

- For some experiencers, it may be easier and more natural to recreate what they remember of their contact events by drawing, painting or sculpting, instead of writing - or even a combination of different methods.

Despite the pros and cons, many experiencers report that they wouldn't trade anything for what they discovered when the veil was lifted from their contact memories with the help of therapy or counseling. Many have come to a new understanding of themselves and found a fresh perspective on their lives and the universe as a whole.

But remember that any exploration of memories can lead to both positive and negative developments, and such a decision should be your choice, based on careful consideration of all the pros and cons. Don't let anyone push you into it if you aren't ready and, if you do decide to make that journey, be sure to choose a qualified, competent and ethical counselor or therapist to be your guide.

*"Some of my memories will never return. They are lost -
along with the crippling feeling of defeat and hopelessness.
Not a tremendous price to pay."*

Carrie Fisher

4

Q: Why are ETs here?

This is perhaps the most frequently asked question in the UFO/ET phenomenon. Whether we are true believers or not quite sure, we all want to know why ETs are here, and the answer has both personal and general implications for individual experiencers and humanity as a whole. Why Earth? Why humans? Why cows?

Many theories have been proposed in answer to this question and over the years, in my work as a therapist and researcher, I have encountered quite a few of them. While some make more sense than others, they all may contain a few grains of truth. Here are some of the more interesting theories, in no particular order. Pick your favorite.

The Slave Race Theory

Certain scholars of ancient cultures believe that alien beings came to Earth millennia ago to exploit her natural resources and tampered with the DNA of early humans for the purpose of creating a slave race to harvest those resources. This genetic tampering may have been responsible for the existence of different blood types and the mysterious Rh-negative factor, among other things. The ETs then departed and the remaining humans somehow managed, over generations, to raise themselves from slaves to the dominant species on the planet, possibly with the continuing guidance of the same extraterrestrial beings who originally manipulated their DNA. Proponents of this theory believe that evidence can be found in ancient art, mythology and religions, and while it may be possible that our progenitors did start out digging gold for otherworldly overlords, there is no proof that this theory is true.

The Alien Ark Theory

This is similar to the Slave Race Theory, except instead of coming to Earth to exploit her natural resources, these beings were refugees from a failing planet who came to Earth to begin anew. They brought technology and culture from their world to share with humanity for the purpose of building a civilization here. Or perhaps their destination was elsewhere and they mistakenly landed or crashed on Earth and were unable to leave. But however they came to be here, they interbred with native humans, which had a significant influence on the genetic development and evolution of humanity. If such ETs did arrive here by accident, maybe after a time, rescue parties evacuated them and their technology, which may explain why some of the monumental structures they created are still here, but the machines and technology used to create them are not.

The Lab Rat Theory

In this theory, as in the Slave Race Theory, humanity was manipulated by alien beings, but not to serve as slave labor; instead, as laboratory specimens for study and experimentation, which some people believe is still happening today. Many experiencers report being taken aboard alien ships and subjected to tests and experiments in which ETs gather information about human anatomy and physiology for the purpose of finding cures for ailments and weaknesses in their own races. This theory seems logical, since it closely mirrors how we use laboratory animals on Earth to enhance our own health and vitality. Is it true? Many people believe it is.

The Time Travel Theory

Some alien visitors to Earth say they have traveled through time from the future to help humanity advance technologically and/or spiritually. They claim to be our descendants who have come back to offer guidance and prevent us from destroying life on the Earth and endangering life elsewhere in the galaxy. Experiencers sometimes relate that when they were aboard alien ships, they were shown images of a future Earth ravaged by wars and environmental disasters designed to drive home such warnings. After being exposed to such terrifying scenarios, experiencers may find their attitudes about life and the world radically changed.

The Divide and Conquer Theory

This theory posits that extraterrestrials are here to create unrest by pitting different human groups and races against each other so we will be weak and easily defeated when they invade and conquer Earth. It's true that human history is a long litany of chaos and war, but if ETs are encouraging conflict on Earth to make us more vulnerable to invasion, after all the years they have been here, why haven't they done it by now? Have they been so busy wreaking havoc on other planets that they just haven't had time to finish us off yet? Or could it be that after all the years of watching, they have finally decided we're not worth conquering after all?

The Ascension Theory

A more positive idea is that ETs are here to help humanity attain a higher level of development, to create a peaceful, non-polarized culture and prepare us for admission into some kind of universal or galactic federation or alliance of advanced beings. Proponents of this theory say they are in contact with spiritually advanced ETs, ascended masters, celestials and other galactic beings who claim they are here to guide humanity through the difficulties we are now facing and into a physically and spiritually ascended state. If they are telling the truth, they certainly have their work cut out for them.

The Party World Theory

This theory proposes that Earth is known throughout the galaxy as a party world where ETs come to have sex with humans and drink our liquor. This is a rather unusual theory, but considering the many reports of human-ET activities involving sex, I guess that part could be accurate. On the other hand, I haven't heard any accounts of ETs drinking alcohol, so I'm inclined to say No on that part. But in this field, it's hard to be completely certain of anything, and this theory does have its supporters.

The Galactic Penal Colony Theory

In stark contrast to the Party World Theory, proponents of this theory claim that the Earth was visited in its infancy by ETs who converted it into a galactic penal colony where the souls of beings who have committed criminal acts on other worlds are remanded for punishment. Such souls incarnate into human bodies on Earth (aka experiencers) to serve life-long sentences for their crimes, and controller ETs abduct, torture and experiment on them. This theory goes on to suggest that in some circumstances, a criminal soul can influence its experiencer host to commit criminal acts, and the experiencer will not be free of the soul until the sentence has been served. Supporters of this theory point to the ongoing unrest, violence and criminality on Earth as proof that it's true. A variation on this theory postulates that souls sentenced to this Earth are never free from their punishment, but are reincarnated here endlessly with no means of escape.

The Fallen Angel Theory

According to this theory, ETs are not galactic travelers, celestial beings or human progenitors, but instead, they are angels who were kicked out of heaven for rebelling against God and relegated to Earth to sow misery and torment, and lead mankind into sin and degradation. Believers back up this theory by comparing historical and contemporary descriptions of ET contact to interpretations from the Bible and other religious texts. They see ETs as evil enemies of humanity who lead us away from true religion, and they believe contact with all extraterrestrial beings should be avoided.

The Interdimensional Being Theory

Proponents of this theory believe that not only are beings from other planets visiting Earth, but beings from dimensions near or related to our own are interacting with us as well. The basic concept isn't new, but this theory takes the idea further to propose that some beings commonly believed to be from other planets - including the gray aliens involved in typical night-time abduction events - are not from other planets, but are actually from other dimensions. This may explain some often reported aspects of typical abduction scenarios, such as descriptions of individuals being moved through solid objects, such as walls, or what appear to be portals or openings in space, and how beings and craft appear and disappear suddenly.

The Natural Resource Theory

Proponents of the Slave Race Theory believe alien beings came to Earth to harvest gold, but others believe some otherworldly beings are interested in Earth's water. Photographs have been taken of ET craft with what resemble pipelines or other devices extending from the craft into bodies of water below, possibly drawing water into the ship. Are the aliens taking samples of water for study? Or perhaps they consume the water or use it to power or facilitate the function of their craft? Are the many UFOs that are seen entering and emerging from our oceans or other bodies of water merely taking advantage of the water as cover for their activities, or are they harvesting and exploiting Earth's underwater resources?

The Cultural/Social Resource Theory

Perhaps some extraterrestrials are on Earth to exploit not its natural resources, but its social and cultural resources. The book, *Millennial Hospitality*,[2] by Charles Hall, tells about his contact with the aliens he calls the Tall Whites on the Nellis Range in Nevada. He states that for many years, the U.S. Air Force allowed this group of extraterrestrial beings to build and maintain scout ships that regularly came and went from a hidden base beneath a mountain on the Range to and from orbiting spacecraft on missions throughout the galaxy, in exchange for advanced alien technology and information. In support of those missions, the aliens were supplied with a location in which to maintain their craft and their living. In addition to the alien scientists and technicians, the base was also home to their families, including children, whom Mr. Hall saw on many occasions. Although the Tall Whites did not like to interact with individual humans, they were very interested in Earth society and culture, and were sometimes transported to nearby cities where they were protected and given private access to certain entertainment venues. He also claims that the alien females were particularly fond of human clothing, which they demanded as part of their trade arrangements with the Air Force.

There may be many answers to the question of why ETs are here. Experiencers report interacting with different groups of alien beings with varied motives and agendas, so maybe one or all of the above theories is valid. We won't know for certain until they come out and tell us. In the meantime, this is another forbidden question that remains unanswered.

"The alien beings have come to the abductees from a source that remains unknown to us. We still do not fully grasp their purposes or their methods. It seems clear however, that 'they' have had to come to 'us,' appearing in material form so that we might know them."

John Mack

[2] Hall, Charles James. *Millennial Hospitality*. Charles Hall. 2002.

5

Q: Why me?

It's likely that thousands of humans alive today have had contact with extraterrestrial beings and don't remember or choose to acknowledge the events. But it's unlikely that every human being is an experiencer. Experiencers are unique. And regardless of the nature of their contact, most of them want to know why they were chosen rather than someone else.

Many experiencers believe they were specifically targeted for contact, although they don't consciously know why. But according to data collected by the FREE Study, out of 1,153 individuals who had experienced contact and who responded to the question, *"Did the ETs ever tell you why you were being targeted for contact?"*, 838 said *No* and only 315 said *Yes*.

Contact with extraterrestrial beings is an experience that can reach deeply into an individual's physical, emotional and spiritual life, and even if ETs do share their reasons for being here, often it's easier for an experiencer to bury the memories and knowledge of the events deep in their subconscious mind than to deal with them consciously.

But the question remains - why do certain people experience contact with ETs while others do not? Do ETs exercise specific criteria for selecting which humans to connect with or is it merely random? While we don't know for certain, there are theories, and we may be able to come close to an answer by looking at some possible determinants for why you were chosen and another person wasn't.

Demographics

Unfortunately, looking at demographics for clues is not particularly helpful. According to the few surveys and studies published to date, class, education, geographic location of residence and race or ethnicity don't appear to mark an individual for ET contact. Human-ET contact appears to cut across all those barriers. Some countries report more UFO sightings than others, but don't report statics regarding contact experiences. And while some studies do indicate differences with respect to sex and age, no formal determinations or conclusions have been drawn there either. Unfortunately, to date, demographics yields no clear answer to this question.

Agreements

Many experiencers report that at some point, either before their birth or in early childhood, they made an agreement with a specific ET group or family to complete a mission during their life on Earth. They may not recall the exact details, but they often feel this very strongly and believe the choices they have made in life and the underlying principles they live by are based on that agreement. In addition, they may continue to receive guidance from their ET families or groups in support of their mission via physical or psychic contact throughout their life. Did you make an agreement with an ET group or family to complete a mission during your earthly life? If so, that may be why you are experiencing contact.

Psychological characteristics

Because contact with extraterrestrial beings seems too fantastic to be real, it's easy to assume that experiencers are unable to distinguish between fantasy and reality. According to several accepted studies, however, there is no solid evidence that experiencers are more fantasy prone than other members of the general public. On the whole, people who report seeing UFOs are not stupid, crazy or social outcasts, but many experiencers do describe themselves as being spiritually aware, open-minded and interested in higher consciousness and personal development. Could this way of thinking and believing be an attribute that ETs seek out in the humans they choose to have contact with and one that you possess? If so, perhaps that's why they are drawn to you.

Physiological traits

It appears that specific physiological traits, such as blood type and genetic history, may be factors in why extraterrestrial beings are interested in certain humans. This may account for reports that contact frequently runs in families. There is also some indication that individuals with Rh-negative blood may be more likely to have contact with ETs and that the condition may actually exist as a result of genetic manipulation of humans in our ancient past. If members of your family are experiencers and if you have Rh-negative blood, that may explain why you have been chosen for contact.

Human-alien hybrids

Some individuals believe they are not only participants in contact events, they are actually products of interbreeding between humans and extraterrestrial beings - human-alien hybrids. In a human-alien hybrid, human traits tend to be dominant, but it is common for the individual to exhibit physiological and anatomical traits and conditions that members of their human family do not. In addition, hybrids may exhibit advanced mental and psychic abilities and the ability to receive communications or downloads of information from their ET families or groups. Although some hybrids report that they have been in conscious communication with their ET families from birth or early childhood, others say they didn't know who they were until later in life when it was revealed to them. If you are experiencing ET contact, is it possible that you are part human and part ET?

ETs incarnating as humans

For most Ufologists in the western world, the subject of incarnation belongs to the realm of religion. But some individuals believe they are actually alien souls incarnated in human form on Earth. Similar to human-alien hybrids, these beings have a purpose for taking on human lives which they may be aware of from childhood or not until later in life.

In her book, *Human by Day, Zeta by Night: A Dramatic Account of Greys Incarnating as Humans,* [3] Judy Carroll tells the story of her life as an alien soul incarnated in a human body. She had a normal human childhood and didn't discover that she was different from others around her until she was an adult, when she had a sudden and shocking realization of the truth. Now she is a normal, happy woman with a job and a family who writes and teaches about the relationship between extraterrestrial beings and humans. But at night, when her body goes to sleep, her soul leaves and travels to a spaceship where she works with her alien family in their mission to assist the awakening of human consciousness to higher levels of awareness. If her story sounds familiar to you and you think it's possible that you, too, are an alien soul in a human body

---

[3] Carroll, Judy. *Human by Day, Zeta by Night: A Dramatic Account of Greys Incarnating as Humans.* Wild Flower Press. 2011.

with a mission on Earth, that may explain why you are in contact with extraterrestrial beings.

Messages

Many experiencers report receiving information and messages from alien beings during contact experiences and some believe they serve as messengers or liaisons between ETs and mankind, to help humanity understand why alien groups are on Earth and how we can benefit from their presence here. The information may come to them in the form of psychic contact or downloads of information either during contact or later, and may deal with everything from science and technology to social and political information, knowledge germane to nature and life on Earth, and advice and guidance personally relevant to specific individuals.

The messengers then relay this information to humanity through various means. Some work as healers, therapists or teachers, some share their messages through the arts and music, and some communicate ET information as writers - essentially, through whatever method they feel can best serve humanity.

The FREE Study reported the following responses to four of their questions about alien messages:

> *"Did the ETs impart reassuring messages to you?"* Out of 1,168 responses, 710 experiencers said *Yes.*

> *"Did the ETs provide a spiritual message to you?"* Out of 1,176 responses, 631 experiencers said *Yes.*

> *"Did the ETs give a message of Love or Oneness to you?"* Out of 1,214 responses, 663 experiencers said *Yes.*

> *"Did the ETs give you an environmental message regarding Earth?"* Out of 1,192 responses, 465 experiencers said *Yes.*

Were you chosen to relay messages from extraterrestrial beings to Earth? If so, that may be why you are experiencing contact.

So why were you chosen?

You may never know the answer to this question, for sure, unless the ETs you are in contact with tell you. But I believe many experiencers, in their deepest heart-of-hearts, do know the answer, even though they may not be consciously aware of it. It is an important question, though, not just for individual experiencers, but for everyone. If you don't know the answer and you want to, keep asking, be patient with yourself, keep your mind and heart open, and don't accept any answer that doesn't sound like truth to you. Like all the other forbidden questions, there is an answer - it just may take a while to find.

"They are the chosen ones who have surrendered.
Once they were particles of light, now they are
the radiant sun!"

Rumi

6

Q: What about implants?

Some individuals believe that objects have been implanted in their bodies during contact with alien beings. These objects are not souvenirs of all contact events, but they are reported often enough to be considered standard items in some ET toolboxes.

The FREE Study asked the question, *"Do you believe that extraterrestrials placed a permanent foreign object (an implant) in your body?"* Out of 1,222 individuals who responded, 630 said *Yes*.

What are they?

Not surprisingly, most suspected alien implants turn out to have earthly origins and usually prove to be run-of-the-mill things like insect bites, skin lesions or natural or man-made objects that become embedded in the body during the course of daily life. Generally, the deciding factors about whether an object is an alien implant are (1) if it appeared in connection with a UFO sighting or an ET encounter, and (2) if it cannot be explained naturally. Even if an experiencer doesn't remember having an implant placed in his body by an alien being, if there was a contact event around the time the object was discovered and there was no natural explanation for the presence of the object, the odds of it being an alien implant rise significantly.

Alien implants reportedly come in a variety of shapes and sizes and may remain in an individual's body until they either disappear on their own or until they are removed by the human subject or by the ETs who placed them there. Although most people who report having implants say they don't suffer ill effects from them, some do have pain and discomfort in the area, can feel the object emitting heat or other types of energy, or have health problems that clear up after the implant has been removed.

Implants have been found in nearly every part of the body, including the arms and legs, the back, neck and behind the ears. They are also sometimes found in natural body openings, areas from which experiencers often report bleeding after contact. Even though it's impossible to verify, the locations of implants are probably related to their function. For instance, behavior modification implants would most likely be placed in or around the brain, drug release implants would probably be placed in muscular areas of the body such as the thighs, and tracking implants could be placed anywhere.

Methods of placing implants into the body may vary, depending on the type of implant and location. In natural body openings, such as the ears, nose and mouth, implants could be inserted non-invasively; however, in other areas, insertion of implants would require surgery using needles or laser scalpels that would leave behind only faint scars. Aliens may also have methods of transporting an implant into an individual's body using the same or similar technology they use to move whole bodies through solid objects.

In some individuals, a bump or bruise forms on the surface of the skin above the implant site, rashes, marks or scars may appear, or there may be burning or itching in the area that may disappear over time or remain permanently. Areas of fluorescence can sometimes be detected when the area around an implant is exposed to a black light. Implants are usually small, ostensibly to fit into tight body spaces and be less liable to detection. They also may be small because alien technology is so advanced that they don't need to be large to be effective.

Individuals who believe they have implants in their heads have reported experiencing certain forms of tinnitus, especially intermittent clicking, buzzing and static noise with no other logical sources, hearing an audible voice in their head that was not their own, sinus problems and chronic nosebleeds.

The late Dr. Roger Leir[4] reported that in regard to several of the implants he removed:

> *"The tissues surrounding these small metallic foreign objects, which looked like 'cantaloupe seeds radiating small tendrils,' were invariably devoid of any inflammatory reaction and were found, inexplicably, to contain nerve proprioceptors . . . no way do these things exhibit the characteristics normally seen with foreign*

---

[4] Roger K. Leir (1934-2014) - American podiatric surgeon, Ufologist and author best known as an investigator of alien implants.

bodies which find their way, through accident or other means, into the human organism." Dr. Roger Leir

He also noted that some of the implants were surrounded by a dense, fibrous membrane that appeared to be made of the individual's own skin. Was such membranous material the body's natural attempt to reject the implant or was it a feature of the implant itself designed to cushion and support it for long-term retention in the body?

Dr. Leir went on to state that of eight suspected alien implants he removed from eight different individuals, all the objects were found on the left side of the bodies; seven of the eight emitted a powerful electromagnetic field easily detectable with a gauss meter; when removed from the body, all seven specimens inexplicably fluoresced under a UV black light; and during laboratory analysis, the objects were complex and contained a diversity of elements (Al, Ba, Ca, Cu, Fe, Mg, Mn, Na, Ni, Ph, Si, Zn) not normally found together in natural objects on Earth. Unfortunately, we do not have a great deal of standard scientific information about implants, because despite the work done by Dr. Leir and others, few suspected implants have been recovered, preserved and thoroughly examined under controlled conditions.

Reportedly, some implants are made of materials that can be detected by X-rays, scans and metal detectors, and some can affect the operation of electronic devices, such as radios and medical equipment. Some less frequently reported types are described as possessing mineral or crystalline structures that are undetectable, and others are described as biological seed-type objects that may merge with an individual's central nervous system and be impossible to remove without risking the health or life of the individual.

Another type of implant may be non-physical - etheric or astral in nature - existing on the subtle energy level, next to physical reality in a kind of hidden "subspace" that cannot be seen or detected with our five physical senses. If such non-physical implants exist, they would most likely be utilized by quasi-physical and non-physical beings not in the physical body, but in the subtle energy body (aura, chakras, meridians). Such beings might also implant or attach a piece of their own energy to a person in order to track them, if possible. Alien non-physical implants would be very advanced. As with physical implants and the physical body, the locations of non-physical implants would be tied to the part of the subtle energy body that corresponds to the behavior or result desired and might be inserted into the body or attached to it by psychic or occult methods.

Living implants

The types of alien implants removed by Dr. Leir were made of metal or mineral, and those utilized by Adrian Dvir's ETMTs were copies of human biological tissue, but living biological and genetic material is also frequently reported being utilized as implants. In human-alien hybridization programs, many female experiencers report being implanted with alien-fertilized human ova and subsequently carrying and giving birth to hybrid children. Some of these individuals also report having alien or human-alien hybrid fetuses implanted into their wombs which they carry to term or near term, and then being returned to a ship or facility where the fetus is removed. Not all pregnancies of this type are successful, ending in false pregnancies or miscarriages, which is probably why many women involved in these procedures report being taken repeatedly.

What are they for?

In his book, *X3: Healing, Entities and Aliens,*[5] Adrian Dvir wrote that the ET medical teams (ETMTs) he worked with utilized implants made from materials they created and brought to Earth with them. The implants were used on humans in various healing applications, and the biomimetic material was designed to bond with the human patient's damaged or ailing body tissue, healing and strengthening it. The implant would remain active in the body for the rest of the individual's life or dissolve when the affected body part had healed, depending on the desired result.

> *"The way the ETMTs did was they always worked with a human healer to monitor the human patient. This wasn't abduction, the patients were always fully aware of where they were and had asked for treatment and it wasn't usually done on a ship. The ETMTs didn't speak directly to the patient, so my job was to observe the procedure and explain it to the patient and relay prescriptions or follow-up instructions from the team to the patient after it was*

---

[5] Dvir, Adrian. *X3: Healing, Entities and Aliens.* Adrian Dvir. 2000.

done. On several occasions when I was assisting, I saw the ETMTs remove diseased or malfunctioning internal organs and treat them with different types of equipment including a special material that looked like tissue paper. They would wrap the organ in the material and then return it to the person's body or sometimes they would use the material to line a body cavity. The teams that I worked with brought everything with them. I have seen this material used in many different ways. We don't have anything like it on Earth." MF

Some researchers and experiencers believe alien implants are used to monitor the location and activity of the human host, maybe to locate them for future encounters, to communicate with them or control them, or to track the results of experiments. They may also be used for monitoring the biological status of individuals involved in hybrid breeding programs. Implants have also been reported being used for the treatment of various injuries and diseases. Some types of implants function automatically and some require the host to activate them.

"I received my implant one evening while I was sitting on the couch in my living room. It had been a bad headache day and I was about to grab my third dose of pain meds when I decided to ask for help. I already had a relationship with an ET family so I closed my eyes, relaxed and mentally reached out and asked them to come and fix my messed-up sinuses if they could. Within a few moments, I felt surrounded by gentle beings and I felt a light touch on my forehead and felt them place a small object in my head between my eyebrows. There was no pain. They said they had put an implant in my head that would be there as long as I needed it and the energy would stop my sinus headaches by preventing inflammation that caused the pain. They said to touch the area on my forehead and visualize it radiating light and it would activate. I touched it and I felt warmth radiating out from the spot throughout my sinuses. I could feel my face light up from the inside-out like a jack-o-lantern and the pain gradually went away and I fell into a restful sleep. Since then when I start to get a headache, I activate the implant and I have fewer and less severe sinus infections and headaches. The

implant is still in my head, I can activate it any time I need it and it's obviously working. There are no negative side-effects and it's free - what could be better than that?" GF

Do ETs monitor their implants?

Some experiencers report being given implants and told they would be monitored and contacted again, but not having conscious recall of further contact. However, with their advanced technology, it may be possible for ETs to monitor implants without an individual's knowledge. Others report that their implants are regularly checked, replaced and sometimes removed completely when they are taken or during visits without actually being taken.

What happens if an implant is removed?

Some experiencers who have had implants removed by human doctors report that contact has stopped, while others report that contact has continued. It seems to be an individual thing. ETs do sometimes remove their own implants, probably depending on why they were put there in the first place and if their purpose is done. Some individuals have reported that after an implant was removed, they initially felt sick, but within a few days or weeks, they felt better and, in some cases, even better than at any other time in their life. But whether an alien implant proves to be problematic or not, it's understandable that most people who have one would want to be rid of it as soon as possible. That doesn't apply to every person or every type of implant, however.

Milab implants

Some individuals who have been subjected to military abductions (milabs) believe they may have received implants as part of those programs, and such implants may be similar to alien implants in their structure, function and loci of placement in the body. While most extra-terrestrial-human communication seems to be telepathic, human milab perpetrators lack telepathic communication methods, so physical devices would be needed. However, those devices might be very advanced and capable of, among other things, monitoring biological states, behavior modification, inducing tiredness, discombobulation, urges and compulsions. They may also be used for timed release of drugs intended to enhance or alter biological states (hormones, immune system, etc.) and for the transmission of voice, text or other signals. Another possible use may be subconscious programming - for example, hypnotic scripts that can be recited while one is sleeping and dreaming, or for harassment while an individual is awake.

What to do

If you think you have an implant and you want it removed, but you don't know who to go to, a UFO investigative group or experiencer therapist may be able to refer you to a doctor with experience in this area and give you guidance on how the implant should be handled and preserved once it has been removed. If an implant is causing you serious medical problems, don't wait - see a doctor as soon as possible. Even if the doctor doesn't believe it's an alien implant, it belongs to you, so you can ask for it and take it to a UFO investigative group for study, sell it on the internet or do whatever you want with it. At least it will be out of your body and, hopefully, any discomfort it caused will be over.

Much has been published about alien implants by individuals who believe they have them and by skeptics who claim they don't exist. But until we are able to confer openly with the beings who are supposedly utilizing them, the subject of implants will remain another forbidden question.

"Whether these objects eventually turn out to be of extraterrestrial or terrestrial origin is not as important as the fact that their technology is highly advanced and they were placed in people unknowingly, against their will."

alienjigsaw.com

7

Q: Did my contact experiences really happen?

A typical abduction event begins in familiar surroundings, but quickly transforms into a bizarre reality where an individual finds himself in a strange place, face to face with alien beings who have taken control of his body and mind without explanation or permission. He then may be subjected to physical, mental and emotional stimuli beyond anything he has experienced before, even in his most terrifying dreams, and in an instant, find himself back in the world from which he was taken, alone, abandoned and confused. Understandably, few people will emerge from something like that unaffected, and even fewer will retain accurate memories of the experience.

Even in positive contact scenarios, the transition from a normal environment to an alien locale, interactions with fantastical beings, and the transition back into everyday reality is often overwhelming. One experiencer likened it to being "chewed up and spit out. When it's over it feels like things weren't put back together quite right." Another said it's "like having your mind turned inside out and back in again. You're never the same." Even when a person is pretty sure that what he experienced really did happen, the effort to recall and understand it is still likely to be a stretch. So it's not surprising that an experiencer may wonder if what he remembers really happened, even if he explores those contact events through formal therapy or counseling.

Getting help to remember

In experiencer therapy, hypnosis is one of the tools commonly used to help individuals recall memories of contact experiences. While hypnosis is safe and effective when utilized correctly in a therapeutic setting, sometimes individuals wonder if what they recalled in a hypnotherapy session was a true memory or a product of their imagination. That's a valid question. The human mind is a fantastic, energetic machine. I doubt that there is anything else like it in the universe, and I'm convinced that is one of the reasons alien beings are so interested in us. But it is also very complex, with lots of twists and turns that make it a challenge to understand and track.

When hypnosis is used to recover memories, an individual is assisted to physically relax, then guided into a highly focused state of mind, similar to deep meditation, in which memories may easily be accessed. Not everyone agrees on the details, but simply put, hypnosis involves two parts of the mind - the conscious mind and the subconscious mind.

The conscious mind is a thought-generator, responsible for reasoning, thinking and making judgments, that is active when you're awake. It's also the place where information, sensory data and memories are combined to create new ideas, where your imagination lives and where fantasies are created. The subconscious mind is also active when you're awake, but it usually takes a back seat to the conscious mind. Sensory data that passes into the conscious mind and thoughts created there are sent to the subconscious mind where they remain until they are either recalled or forgotten. Because it's not a thought-generator, the subconscious mind doesn't have the ability to create new ideas or fantasies.

When you're awake, memories can emerge from your subconscious mind in response to requests from your conscious mind or when they are triggered by new sensory data entering your conscious mind. When you're asleep and your conscious mind is taking a break, memories may emerge from your subconscious mind during dreaming. Sometimes they are organized and make sense, but most of the time they are a jumbled-up mess. Memories are not dangerous and they can't harm you; however, they often have emotions attached to them that can be disturbing and make them difficult to make sense of. Hypnosis encourages your body and conscious mind to relax and allow memories to emerge in an organized way. A competent therapist will not tell you what to remember, but will guide you and help you organize what you remember into a picture of your experience that makes sense and has meaning to you. You are the person who had the experience, so the memories must have meaning to you, not the therapist or anyone else.

So, back to the question - did the event you remembered in hypnosis really happen or did you make it up?

When you are in a deep hypnotic trance, accessing your subconscious mind, you won't be able to create fantasies because your subconscious mind can't do that. But if you don't achieve a deep enough trance, your conscious mind may still be awake enough to create fantasies, and then you'll be faced with the task of separating those fantasies from authentic memories of what you really experienced. This sometimes happens, but if it does, a qualified therapist can help you work through it.

What I remembered in hypnosis was like a book I read. How do I know if I was just remembering the book?

Your subconscious mind has a huge storage capacity, but it's not limitless, so over time you either forget memories or they become inaccessible. If the memory of the book you read is still in your subconscious, either because you recently read it or because it has been retained as a memory for some other reason, it could be part of what you recalled in your hypnosis session. However, it's also possible that you chose to read that particular book because it reminded you of a prior contact event you had, and when it came up in the hypnosis session, it was a true memory of that event. This happens quite frequently. I know it sounds a bit convoluted, but that's how memories behave; sometimes they stay buried for years and then emerge, inexplicably, when something triggers them.

False memories

"False memories" are generally defined as memories of events that didn't really happen. But technically, there is no such thing as a false memory, because everything you experience is stored in your subconscious mind as a memory, without being labeled true or false. Your subconscious mind does not make judgments about the truth or accuracy of the data stored there - it merely stores it. However, during the process of recalling something, either on your own or in hypnosis, sometimes memories can get mixed together and muddle up the original memory, or your conscious mind can distort an original memory. The memories are not false, they're just no longer the original memories. In addition, it's possible that during a hypnosis session, information can be introduced or suggestions can be made that might distort or color memories. But if you work with a well-trained and experienced therapist, that can be avoided.

Additionally, individuals suffering from certain mental illnesses (schizophrenia, dissociative identity disorder and schizotypal personality disorder, etc.) may distort or fabricate recollections of events that did not actually happen and, in those situations, the term false memories may apply. Confabulation is also a type of false memory that results from neurological dysfunction. All of these are related to serious mental issues, and any experiencer suffering from them should be under the care of a medical professional.

The truth is that recovering specific memories of ET contact can be a tricky, lengthy process and, in some cases, might not even be possible. Human memory is notoriously undependable. Even if you already have partial recall of a contact event and decide to go ahead with therapy to get more information or fill in the gaps, you may discover that it actually happened differently from how you remembered it up until then. In the end, you will have to do the work, but a skilled, experiencer therapist can help you feel confident that what you do remember actually happened.

A word of caution

If any therapist or counselor tells you they have the ability to recover memories, make abductions stop or accomplish anything else for 100% of the people, 100% of the time, beware. Therapy can be very helpful, but no one - short of a genuine saint or miracle-worker - can give that kind of guarantee and actually make good on it. Of course, it's your life to do with what you will, but I hope you won't let anyone take advantage of you.

Many people wonder if what they remembered in hypnosis was a real memory or not. My general rule of thumb is this: if you made it up and if you're honest with yourself, you will know you made it up. You might not want to admit it to yourself or the therapist, but you will know. If you think you might have made it up, but you aren't sure, then you most likely didn't, and your memory is genuine.

"Let go of the need to control. Trust the process. Trust your intuition. Trust yourself."

lovetweal.com

8

Q: Are all contacts like mine?

While the vast number of human-ET contact scenarios are similar in some respects, no two are exactly the same. Each person perceives and processes his contact experience through his own brain and personality that are unlike any other brain and personality in the universe. Two individuals can go through the same contact event and perceive it differently. This produces experiences that run the gamut from traumatic and horrifying to blissful, uplifting and life-affirming - sometimes even humorous - and it's one of the reasons contact with alien beings is so difficult to quantify and prove.

There is almost certainly more going on in the area of human-ET contact interactions on Earth than anyone is aware of, but there are some commonly reported types. Although they possess similarities and differences, they are all valid contact experiences.

Alien abduction

This is the most well-known kind of contact, most often represented in the media and entertainment. The term describes an event in which a person is taken against his or her will by alien or otherworldly beings and then returned at a later time. This type of event may involve an individual being subjected to physical examinations, experiments and tests, reproductive procedures, educational activities or being given messages to relay back to specific individuals or humanity as a whole. Abductions can take place at any time, but are most often reported at night, there may or may not be prior warnings, and sleep paralysis is often, but not always involved. The human subject of alien abduction may be conscious or unconscious during the experience and may have full memory, partial memory or no memory afterward. While not all abduction experiences are the same, typical scenarios are reported, and the aftermath of an abduction experience may be negative or positive.

Taking

This is similar to abduction, except the person is not taken against his or her will. More and more occurrences of this type of contact event are now being reported. There may or may not be prior warnings that the event is going to happen and the person may or may not remember it later. While there may be some elements of fear or discomfort, these events are often described, overall, as uplifting and conferring a feeling of blessing or being chosen for a special purpose. There may be long periods of time between the takings, sometimes years. While scenarios tend to vary more in this type of event than in typical abductions, usually they are positive, and experiencers often look forward to future occurrences.

Visit

This is the most commonly reported type of human-ET contact experience and the most varied. Typically, it takes place when an experiencer wakes up in his bed at night and sees non-human beings in the room with him, but it can happen anywhere, anytime, and the aftermath can be positive or negative. During a visit, there may be communication between the human and the alien beings and/or downloads of information. Physical contact is sometimes reported that may include healing of the human by the alien beings, but the experiencer is not removed from the location. Visits also include events in which ETs or ET craft appear in response to an individual or group's signal or request for contact.

Programmed event

In a programmed event, an individual receives instructions from an ET or group to appear at a specific location on a certain date and time, and the individual may be allowed to bring others with him. Experiences at the contact site are reported to vary from physical sightings of craft and actual ET entities to psychic contact and takings. There may be telepathic contact between the alien entity and human attendees, downloads of information or only visual contact.

Psychic contact

In this type of event, ETs make contact with a person when he or she is in a meditative, prayerful or highly-suggestible state of mind; however, it can happen any time, including dreaming, and no physical contact or transport is involved. Typically, this is done for the purpose of downloading information from ET to human, exchange of information between the two or preparing the human contactee for future events. This type of contact is becoming more and more frequent, and many adult experiencers who began having physical contact as children now report that as adults, they have only psychic contact, which they describe as much easier and more enjoyable than their earlier physical experiences.

Contact dream

Many experiencers describe having dreams of contact with extraterrestrial beings - on ships, on other planets or in other dimensions. But for some people, those dreams are unusually vivid and as real as everyday reality itself, and may actually constitute a form of psychic contact. Contact dreamers often describe experiences that are similar or exactly like those described by physical abductees and contactees, with the exception that the dreamer remains asleep during the event and is not removed from his or her bed. A contact dreamer may talk in their sleep, describing what they are seeing, or speak languages they are hearing or speaking in the dream, and may later remember information that was imparted to them during the dream. They may even awaken with marks on their bodies which were apparently acquired during activities that took place during the dream. While there is no explanation for this type of contact, because it takes place while an individual is sleeping and their conscious mind is at rest, perhaps they are somehow tapping into a level of consciousness they are unable to access during waking. Or perhaps ETs are manipulating or accessing the dreamer's brain while he or she is in a dream state.

The FREE Study reported the following response to their question, *"Did you have an encounter with an ET (non-human intelligent being) but the ET was not physically present?"* Out of 1,632 responses, 1,141 said *Yes.*

Encounter

Encounters are unplanned, unexpected meetings with extraterrestrial or otherworldly beings. They may involve situations where individuals accidentally come upon a landed or crashed alien craft or the opening to an underground base in a remote location, but it's possible to have unexpected encounters with alien beings anywhere, even in public places. Alien beings performing missions on Earth may be cautious and well disguised, but they're not infallible, and they do sometimes end up in the wrong places. A friend of mine tells about an encounter she had with a poorly-disguised and obviously out-of-place ET one winter evening near the entrance to a major department store in Phoenix, Arizona.

One of the most well-known encounter experiences happened to Carl Higdon in 1974. While elk hunting in Medicine Bow National Forest, Wyoming, he unexpectedly came upon five elk standing together in a clearing. He took aim with his rifle and fired, but immediately felt a "zone of strangeness" surround him and the elk. The sound of the shot seemed to come from faraway, time seemed to slow down, and Higdon could see the bullet as it left the gun, traveled slowly through the air and fell to the ground about sixty feet away without striking any of the animals. As he went to retrieve the bullet, an odd-looking humanoid figure dressed in black appeared and gave him a "pill," telling him it would alleviate his hunger for four days. He was then taken aboard a spaceship, transported to their home world and, after being told that they couldn't use him, returned to the forest several hours later, weak and in a state of disarray. When he finally made it back to his truck, he was eight miles from where he had started. There are many other interesting details in this story, including the healing of a serious medical condition that had plagued Higdon for a long time, but it's a classic case of an unplanned alien encounter. Many other types of encounters have been reported throughout the years.

When encounters occur, experiencers often mention missing time or a feeling of being "out of time and place" which may linger for up to several hours afterward. Memories of an encounter may return shortly after the event or not until years later.

Aliens as co-workers

I don't remember seeing this job description at Career Day when I was in high school, but some humans say they have worked with otherworldly beings in high-security government or military facilities on Earth. In some situations, the aliens were there by choice, and in others, against their will. In addition to Charles Hall's claims of working with the Tall Whites on the Nellis Range in Nevada, there are other claims of underground facilities where aliens and human scientists and military personnel work together. Needless to say, these activities are hush-hush and their very existence is controversial, even within the government and UFO community.

Milab (military abduction)

Milabs are similar to ET abductions, but instead of extraterrestrials, experiencers are reportedly abducted by humans disguised as ETs, controlled by government or military organizations. The experiencer may be taken to an Earth or off-world facility for various purposes once or multiple times. In some cases, alien beings are involved or present as observers. Often, the person taken in the milab has had prior genuine extraterrestrial contact, which may be the reason he or she was chosen for the milab abduction. These encounters are usually described as unpleasant.

Milabs are not reported in great numbers. The FREE Study noted the following response to their question, *"Do you recall ever having what is commonly called a 'Military Abduction' or MILAB, where humans abducted you?"* Out of 1,275 responses, only 157 said *Yes*. But some investigators believe that genuine extraterrestrial beings do not abduct humans and that all abductions are actually milabs.

In their book, *Beyond Strange: True Tales of Alien Encounters and Paranormal Mysteries,*[6] Bob and Trish MacGregor tell the story of Connie Cannon, who was driving to St. Augustine Beach, Florida, with her son, John, when they may have been involved in a milab:

> *"They were about 100 miles south of Atlanta on I-75 in daylight when suddenly Connie was confused about her location. She was no longer on the interstate but she was certain she hadn't taken an exit. Yet, she and her son were now driving on a strange grid of roads with no buildings in sight. The next thing she knew, she and her son were on their knees outside their vehicle, on a black asphalt tarmac near airplane hangars, sobbing hysterically. Circling overhead were several noisy choppers and three round, softly grumbling spacecraft. In front of her and John were a group of grays and several military men in fatigues and heavy boots who held massive-looking assault weapons. The grays seemed to be just loitering in the area, but one of the soldiers pointed an assault weapon directly at Connie and, in a menacing tone warned her, "If you ever*

---

[6] MacGregor, Bob & Trish. *Beyond Strange: True Tales of Alien Encounters and Paranormal Mysteries.* Crossroads Press. 2017.

. . . you will never see your family again." Then suddenly she and her son were back in the car - although she had no memory of actually getting into the car - and everyone else was gone, and her son had fallen asleep. She started up the car and drove off as fast as she could away from the area, but, exhausted, she found herself driving around a labyrinth of roads, not knowing where she was. Finally, she came upon a convenience store and stumbled inside and when she told the clerk that she'd gotten lost off the I-75, the clerk told Connie that she was on Warner Robins Air Force Base and couldn't get off the base without going through the same gate she had come in through. Connie had no memory of entering any gate and had no idea she was on a military facility. When they finally got home, three hours later than expected, both Connie and her son were exhausted and immediately went to bed. Later, her son remembered being lost and frightened, but he couldn't remember why and he didn't feel normal for the next few days. He has never remembered the details of the event but he is certain that something awful happened."

There is some evidence that not all milabs are perpetrated by elements of the military, but actually by covert intelligence management groups that merely utilize military or paramilitary personnel and facilities to abduct humans who have had previous contact with genuine ETs. The purpose of such groups would likely be to gather information about the ETs the human subjects have had past contact with, not the humans themselves.

The mystery of milabs is one of the most controversial in the human-ET contact phenomenon, but while no one seems to know the truth, something is obviously going on. There is more information about milabs in the Appendix section of this book.

The human-ET contact phenomenon is complex and varied, and all scenarios, be they abductions, takings, visits, psychic contact, encounters, working with ETs, milabs or others, constitute valid contact. Your experiences may be similar to others or completely different, but that doesn't make them any more or less real. There is no right or wrong when it comes to human-ET contact experiences. They are all unique and remarkable, just like the people who experience them.

Q: Are all contacts like mine?

"Here is the mystery - can we attribute the differences in contact types to the actions of the extraterrestrials or the humans involved? This is an important question and one that remains unanswered."

Donald Spencer

9

Q: Why don't I remember my ET contacts?

The human mind is an amazing landscape that has never been fully plotted, and part of that landscape is memory. We all experience it, generally, in the same way, but no one really understands how it works, and in the field of human-ET contact, that is especially true. Some individuals have clear, conscious memories of their contact/abduction experiences, but most have only partial, vague recollections of theirs.

> *"I used to have these memories, really just bits and pieces of memories that I could never quite put together into a coherent whole. I knew they had to do with something that had happened to me when I was a kid that involved floating through the night sky and sounds and odd smells and beings that were there in the background, and they always ended with me being dropped down into my bed. They weren't really frightening, just strange and like on the tip of my brain but I couldn't remember them. Finally, I decided to get serious and ask for help, and was able to put together the pieces, but it wasn't easy and it took a long time. I learned a lot. It changed me."* PT

Simply put, memory is the human mind's method of storing information. On the face of it, conscious memory of contact events might seem advantageous, but when those events are traumatic, many experiencers would give anything not to remember them. Conscious recollection doesn't necessarily make the aftermath of an event easier to live with; indeed, remembering may actually make it worse.

Psychologists don't agree on all the details of why individuals remember certain things and not others, and there is no clear and universally accepted theory of the process. However, most experts accept some basic reasons why you may not remember certain events that take place in your life, including ET contact events.

You forgot

We all know how frustrating it is to forget something that later we want or need to know, and the knowledge that forgetting is a natural function of our mind doesn't make it any less frustrating when it happens.

In humans, all input from the physical senses passes through the central nervous system and ends up in the brain, where it is categorized according to its importance and then moved into the subconscious mind to either be accessed later or forgotten. Basically, forgetting is the spontaneous and gradual "disremembering" of information that has been stored in the subconscious mind. There are two popular explanations for forgetting. One explanation is that over time, the subconscious mind releases unneeded stored information through the process of forgetting, and once that information has been forgotten, it's gone forever and cannot be retrieved. The other explanation is that once information is moved into the subconscious mind, it remains there for the life of the individual, but the ability to retrieve it can be degraded or lost over time. This means that even though memories of your ET contact event may still be in your subconscious mind, you might not be able to recover them.

Your memory was repressed

A repressed memory is a memory that has been unconsciously blocked by your mind. This is also known as "motivated forgetting," a process in which you purposely don't remember something because it's too painful to deal with consciously. The protective powers of your mind are formidable, enabling it to repress anything that it believes is too traumatic for you to cope with. But repressed memories can behave like time bombs, remaining undetected in the subconscious indefinitely and emerging when least expected. This is why experiencers can sometimes go for years after contact without remembering anything, and then unexpectedly start recalling bits and pieces or floods of information about past contact events. Repressed memories may be recoverable, but in the process, other memories may come up along with them that you may not want to remember.

Your memory was blocked

You know that maddening experience when you're trying to think of a word and it's right there on the tip of your tongue, but you just can't get it out of your mouth? Psychologists call this a "TOT" (tip-of-the-tongue) memory block. It's a kind of glitch that arises between your brain and your mouth, it's not normally serious and if you're patient, you'll usually find the word you're looking for before long. That type of memory block is natural, temporary and explainable in terms of everyday mind/body function.

However, in the case of human-ET contact, the term "memory block" is often used to describe something different. While a repressed memory and a TOT memory block are natural functions of the human mind, many experiencers report that during contact, a device or instrument was used on them, creating a block that prevented them from later recalling memories of what happened. If you experienced a memory block that resulted from ET contact, the memory may still be in your subconscious mind and you may be able to recall it, but there is no guarantee.

Your memory was erased

Memory erasure is defined as "the selective artificial removal of memories or associations from the mind." Research into memory erasure has been done to benefit patients suffering from psychiatric disorders such as post-traumatic stress disorder and substance use disorder. This type of research has been done in the public eye, but there have long been claims of covert government and military mind control and personality alteration experiments in which memory erasure techniques have been developed and tested.

Additionally, some experiencers report that certain alien beings they have encountered possess technology that can erase human memories. If a memory of an ET contact event has been erased, regardless of who erased it, it's probably no longer recoverable, unless the ETs have the technology and choose to do so.

So, if you don't remember your contact experience, did you forget it or was the memory repressed, blocked or erased? If you forgot it or it was erased, then it's most likely gone and unrecoverable. If it was repressed or blocked, you may be able to remove the block and retrieve the memory. But before doing so, you should seriously consider why the memory was repressed or why the block was put there and whether or not you really want to face what might emerge once it has been removed. That may be one can of worms better left unopened.

You made an agreement

Many experiencers believe that before their current life, they made an agreement with an extraterrestrial group or family that as part of their mission on Earth, they would willingly participate in activities conducted by them. They may have agreed to be taken for experiments, examinations, tests and procedures that might be painful and traumatic, with the assurance that their bodies would be healed and memories of such encounters would be blocked or erased from their minds so they would have no recollection of the pain and trauma. If you made such an agreement and the ETs you work with have kept their part of the bargain, memories of such activities will be blocked until the time you and the ETs agree to remove the blocks. However, if the agreement was for erasure, such memories are not likely to be recoverable.

You have amnesia

If you're a fan of daytime TV, you have certainly heard of amnesia - or at least the dramatized version of it. Everyone has occasional memory lapses, but amnesia is a type of memory loss in which information about an event that enters the brain is never moved into long-term storage in the subconscious mind, or which is moved into storage, but for some reason is later rendered unrecoverable. It's similar to forgetting, except unlike forgetting, which is usually permanent, amnesia can be either temporary or permanent.

Amnesia can be caused by physical trauma, such as head and brain injuries, use of certain drugs and alcohol or conditions such as Alzheimer's disease. Dissociative amnesia is a type of memory loss that can be caused by traumatic physical, mental or emotional events, including ET contact experiences. Amnesia, even temporary, should be taken seriously and referred to a doctor for accurate diagnosis and treatment.

Dreaming - the mind flush?

Not everyone agrees about the purpose of dreaming, but one theory is that dreaming is the subconscious mind's way of flushing out unneeded information. Because dreams happen when we are unconscious, we can experience all the energy and emotions of real activities without actually doing them - the euphoria of flying without an airplane, the excitement of fighting off a vampire with a swizzle stick, or the thrill of sexual escapades with people we would never even talk to in real life - without danger or repercussions. Dreaming is a lot safer than actually doing and much less embarrassing. Your subconscious mind is a huge storehouse of information, but it doesn't need to hold onto every sensory input it has received since you were in the womb, so dreaming may be the mind's way of clearing out the old stuff and making room for the new. If a memory is flushed out in a dream, including a memory of ET contact, it's most likely gone and irretrievable.

Reliability of memory

Human memory is notoriously unreliable, especially memories of unusual and traumatic events, such as contact with alien beings. Memories are influenced by whatever enters the mind immediately before, during and after an event, and even whatever the person is thinking at the time the event is remembered. Memories are influenced by learning, emotions and physical experiences and, essentially, they are reconstructed every time they are remembered. Memories of contact events do sometimes emerge in bits and pieces or in blocks over time, if triggered by something, but even then, there is no guarantee they will be accurate, so you should always retain a healthy skepticism of them.

There is a belief that memories recalled consciously, without the aid of hypnosis or therapy, are somehow more accurate and dependable than those recalled through therapy, but that is not necessarily true. While it's possible that during a hypnosis session, information can be introduced or suggestions can be made that might distort or color an individual's memories, a qualified and experienced therapist will avoid that and, at the same time, help the individual navigate through whatever memories do come up. Because there are so many things that affect a person's memory, recollections that emerge in therapy are often more accurate than those he or she recalls on their own. Sometimes, contact events that have been remembered consciously are later discovered to be false, so memories recalled through hypnosis or therapy may actually be more accurate than those remembered consciously.

What should you do?

You may remember your contact experiences on your own, however, even when you do, the memories may be incomplete and incomprehensible and in the end, you may decide to get help working through them. If you do, there are options, some healthier and more effective than others. Counseling, therapy and groups are good suggestions. But don't forget that you are not alone, you are probably not crazy, and help is available if you want it.

"Memories are bullets. Some whiz by and only spook you. Others tear you open and leave you in pieces."

Richard Kadrey

10

Q: Am I crazy?

Hundreds, thousands and possibly millions of individuals are convinced that they have had contact with extraterrestrial beings. It's possible that some of those experiences are fantasies or the result of mental disorders, but not all of them. In your situation, I don't know. But one thing is certain, if you are suffering from some form of psychopathology, you will be exhibiting additional signs and symptoms of the disease. If you're experiencing nothing more than a belief that you have been in contact with alien beings, you can probably assume that you're not crazy.

Over the years, mental health professionals and researchers have searched in vain for a relationship between an interest in UFOs and indicators of poor mental health, but to date, none of their interviews with experiencers, surveys or psychometric tests have provided solid evidence that connects the two.

In 1998, researcher June O. Parnell, Ph.D.[7] administered the Minnesota Multiphasic Personality Inventory (MMPI) and the Sixteen Personality Factor Questionnaire (16PFQ) to 225 people who had reported contact with UFOs or ETs. The MMPI is a standard tool for finding psychiatric disorders and the 16PF is an established test for selected personality traits. There were no signs of psychopathology in participants in either test.

Berthold E. Schwarz, M.D.[8] reported that out of 30,000 hospitalized mental patients in New York, none had been institutionalized because of hallucinations or insane beliefs about UFOs or ETs. Schwarz interviewed many UFO witnesses and their families and administered psychological tests such as the MMPI, and in nearly all cases, he described the witnesses as honest, sincere, trustworthy and free of psychiatric issues; although in a few cases, he did find unrelated problems.

---

[7] Parnell, June O., Ph.D. *Journal of UFO Studies*, n.s. 2, , 45-58. J. Allen Hynek Center for UFO Studies. 1990.

[8] Schwarz, Berthold, Eric, M.D. (1924-2010), psychiatrist and researcher into UFO and paranormal activity.

In none of those cases were reports of UFO sightings or contact either the presenting or secondary symptom.

Similarly, in another study, individuals who reported being taken by alien beings were put through a battery of psychological tests by Elizabeth Slater, Ph.D., a trained psychologist. She was not informed that the subjects had all reported experiencing UFO abductions until after she had completed her assessments of the test results. Her conclusion was as follows:

> "The first and most critical question is whether our subjects' reported experiences could be accounted for strictly on the basis of psychopathology, i.e., mental disorder. The answer is a firm no. In broad terms, if the reproductions were confabulated fantasy productions based on what we know about psychological disorders, they could only have come from pathological liars, paranoid schizophrenics and severely and extraordinarily rare hysteroid characters subject to fugue states and/or multiple personality shifts . . . it is important to note that not one of the subjects, based on the test data, falls into any of these categories. Therefore, know, while the testing can do nothing to prove the veracity of the UFO abduction reports, one can conclude that the test findings are not inconsistent with the possibility that reported abductions have, in fact, occurred."[9]

Further exhaustive tests carried out by Caroline McLeod at Harvard in the 1990s, compared forty abduction experiencers with forty matched controls, using a broad range of psychopathology-in-personality measures. Again, the results were unambiguous:

> "No findings of personality disorder or other psychopathology that might explain the abduction phenomenon distinguished the experiencers from the control group."[10]

---

[9] Slater, Elizabeth, Ph.D. *Addendum to Conclusions on Nine Psychologicals, Final Report on the Psychological Test of UFO Abductees.* Fund for UFO Research. 1985.

[10] McLeod, Caroline, et al. *UFO Evidence: A Scientific Study of the UFO Phenomenon and the Search for Extraterrestrial Life.* Psychological Inquiry, Vol. 7, No. 2. 1996.

Three national polls were conducted by The Roper Organization in 1991.[11] Nearly 6,000 people responded to the polls, and the results indicated that 1 out of every 50 adult Americans may have had UFO abduction experiences. In 1991, when the Roper Polls were conducted, 1 out of 50 adult Americans was equivalent to almost 4 million people. While some of the results have since been questioned, responses to the polls showed that: 1 out of every 5 adult Americans had awakened paralyzed with the sense of a strange figure or presence in the room; nearly 1 adult in 8 had experienced a period of 1 hour or more which they apparently lost; 1 adult in 10 had felt the sense of flying through the air without knowing why or how; 1 adult in 10 had seen unusual lights or balls of light in a room without understanding what caused them; and 1 adult in 10 had discovered puzzling scars on his or body without remembering how or where they were acquired.

On the basis of many such surveys and his own direct assessments of the mental health of the many abductees he had personally interviewed, John Mack stated that the verdict was obvious.

> *"Efforts to establish a pattern of psychopathology other than disturbances associated with a traumatic event have been unsuccessful. Psychological testing of abductees has not revealed evidence of mental or emotional disturbance that could account for their reported experiences."*[12]

Fantasy proneness

Because reports of abduction/contact events seem fantastic, it's easy to postulate that the individuals experiencing them have an inability to distinguish between fantasy and reality. However, studies have failed to produce any solid evidence that experiencers are more fantasy prone or suffer more from mental illness than the general population.

In their firsthand study of twenty-seven abduction experiencers,

---

[11] *The Roper Survey,* July-September, 1991. Commissioned by John E. Mack, M.D., Professor of Psychiatry at Harvard Medical School.

[12] John Edward Mack, M.D. (1929 – 2004) - American psychiatrist, author, Professor of Psychiatry at Harvard Medical School.

Rodeghier, Goodpaster and Blatterbauer[13] found that levels of fantasy proneness, as measured by the Inventory of Childhood Memories and Imaginings (ICMI), a validated measure of fantasy proneness, were no higher than fantasy proneness levels in the general population.

Spanos, Cross, Dickson and DuBreuil[14] compared a group of individuals reporting UFO sightings and alien contact to a group of individuals not reporting such experiences. Utilizing the ICMI and other measures of imaginal properties, they found no differences between UFO experiencers and non-experiencers. Spanos, et al., wrote:

> *"These findings clearly contradict the hypothesis that UFO reports - even intense UFO reports characterized by such seemingly bizarre experiences as missing time and communication with aliens - occur primarily in individuals who are highly fantasy prone, given to paranormal beliefs, or unusually suggestible."*

Sleep paralysis

As discussed elsewhere in this book, sleep paralysis is a state in which, during falling asleep or waking from sleep, a person is mentally aware, maybe able to see or hear things going on around him, but be unable to move or speak. It can be terrifying to experience, but it's actually a normal condition that happens to nearly everyone at least once in their lifetime, and to some people chronically. In most cases, it passes after a few minutes and for those who suffer chronically, the condition can usually be managed or alleviated with treatment and therapy.

However, sleep paralysis, or something akin to it, is also a familiar aspect of many alien abduction experiences. However, most reported abduction experiences are different from general reports of sleep paralysis in a number of aspects. First, while in the minority, a portion of abduction experiences do occur during the day while the individual is awake, and these daytime reports are similar to events that occur at night. Second, experiencers show similar phobic reactions to events and material linked to abduction material that are not linked to sleep

---

[13] Rodeghier M., Goodpaster J., Blatterbauer S. *Psychosocial characteristics of abductees: Results from the CUFOS abduction project.* JUFOS, Vol. 3. 1991.

[14] Spanos, N.P., Cross, P.A., Dickson, K., & DuBreuil, S.C., *Close Encounters: An examination of UFO experiencers.* Journal of Abnormal Psychology 102(4), 624-632. 1993.

alone. Third, in experiencers, insomnia, anxiety symptoms and night-mares tend to resolve with the conscious processing of abduction material over time or through counseling or therapy, which would seem unlikely if the traumatic experience was caused by sleep paralysis and not directly linked to contact.

Furthermore, sleep paralysis of long duration tends to be a symptom of narcolepsy, a neurological disorder characterized by an overwhelming desire to sleep at any time. Individuals with narcolepsy may also suffer from cataplexy, a sudden loss of voluntary muscle tone with full consciousness.

> *"Those experiencers who have undergone electro-encephalograph (EEG) testing in an attempt to find a neurological cause for their experiences report no significant findings. Thus, there is no evidence that sleep paralysis can account for the abduction phenomenon."*[15]

The content of contact/abduction stories is so far outside the realm of everyday reality that it naturally seems crazy, and most individuals who have the temerity to speak out about their experiences are destined to face a host of difficulties as a result. If people around you think you're crazy - or if you think you might be - please take care of your mental and physical health and make sure there isn't cause for concern in either of those areas. If there is, get help. It's available for those who want it.

> *"Two possibilities exist: either we are alone in the Universe or we are not. Both are equally terrifying."*
>
> *Arthur C. Clarke*

---

[15] Parnell, June O., Ph.D. *Personality Characteristics on the MMPI, 16PF and ACL of Persons Who Claim UFO Experiences.* University of Wyoming. 1986.

11

Q: Have we met?

We all occasionally run into someone who seems familiar, but who we can't recall by name or remember when or where we met or interacted with before. It's a fairly common experience and if we really need to remember who they are, we usually will, eventually. On the other hand, if it was just a brief encounter that didn't matter, more often than not, we just let it pass and forget it.

But have you ever met someone in your everyday life that you recall seeing aboard an alien craft or during another type of contact event? Many experiencers say they have, and when they see the person again in their everyday life, they may recognize him or her right away, but the memories may be incomplete or unclear, and it may take time to put together the names, faces and places completely.

In a surprisingly large number of instances, once experiencers recall the event completely, whether on their own or through therapy to help them remember, they recognize the others as people with whom they have close relationships in their everyday lives, sometimes even spouses. Unfortunately, connections remembered from contact events don't always carry over well into an experiencer's normal everyday life.

"I recently started a new job. It's a small business and everyone has been friendly and I get along with everyone fine, except one guy. When I first met him I felt like I knew him from somewhere but I couldn't put my finger on it. He never did anything to me, but I was really uncomfortable around him from the beginning, nearly to the point of panic. He was assigned to another office for a month and I forgot about it, but when he came back to our office and spoke to me, that awful panicky feeling was there again. I know I've had ET contacts in the past and I don't remember them all, but after he came back to the office I had a dream and in the dream, I was on a ship or somewhere with ETs in a room with a swimming pool and there was some kind of experiment going on with people being forced to breathe under water. As I watched, a man

came up from under the water screaming and gasping for air. It was the guy from work. The ETs got him out of the pool, but he was in terrible shape and it really shook me up because I was next in line and I didn't know what was gonna happen to me. I don't remember going into the pool, but I woke up from the dream in a panic. I guess that's why I don't feel comfortable around swimming pools or big bodies of water and also why I feel panicky around the guy at work because it makes me remember what happened with the ETs. I don't know if I will ever be able to be around him without feeling panicky." RV

In some cases, female experiencers who recall being part of alien reproductive procedures have been returned to ships where infants or children were presented to them as their hybrid offspring, and the women were asked to hold them or play with them. While these human women may have no memory of impregnation procedures having taken place or of giving birth (possibly due to memory blocks or erasure), they may feel emotional connections to the children and recognize them as their own.

"It's a baby. . . She's bringing a baby to me and I feel that I need to hold it. I feel as if it's important to the baby that it has this and I'm happy to do it. It's very important and they can't do it. It needs it from me. They can't give it what it needs completely. I don't know how I know this, I just understand it. Then they take the baby away and I feel a loss . . . I feel a connection. I feel bonded." JP

Visits aboard the ships may be repeated over time as the children grow up.

Other experiencers report being taken to ships when they were children where they interacted with other children - human, alien and human-alien hybrids - whom they recognized from previous contacts. During such visits, the children often played games and took part in lessons in a variety of subjects taught by alien teachers. Some experiencers who have had multiple contacts say the same beings were present in each contact, acting as tutors or nannies. They often refer to some of the beings as playmates and friends, they know their names, trust them and feel affection for them, which they believe the aliens return.

"My first memories of ETs was when I was 5 or 6 years old. It was night time and I was sleeping on the top bunk bed with my sister on the bottom bunk. I woke up and felt something pulling at my blanket. At first I thought it was my mom, but then I heard a funny voice say "It's time to play!" That sounded good to me so I sat up and before I knew it, I was outside in the back yard and there was a grown-up there who held my hand and we walked through a big hole in the fence, like a cave and came out on the other side in a different place. I don't know where it was but I remember playing all kinds of games with kids who looked different from me. I mean some of them looked really strange but I didn't care. I was having fun. And the grown-up wasn't a human being, but something like a big insect, but very sweet and gentle and I wasn't afraid of her. She was clapping and smiling. When I got older the experiences were different - usually some kind of learning game or test - but the grown-up was always there. I've heard other people talk about how scary their experiences were but mine weren't, I think because I always felt at home there with my ET friends." TR

Why do some contact scenarios involve "ET friends?" The same beings year after year? With children, it makes sense. An ET friend can help get a child started in contact procedures, supervise him, keep him on task during activities and help him feel less afraid. Some adult experiencers say they have seen the same beings on ships since they were children, and they always feel calmer and less fearful when they are there.

In addition to aliens, human-alien hybrids have acted as companions, teachers and guides to experiencers, and such relationships have sometimes developed into intimate physical and romantic relationships that have lasted years.

So, are human-ET friendships real? Is it possible that genuine, lasting friendships do develop between ETs and humans? Or are they merely tools that ETs use to gain our trust and render us easier to control? If we ever get the answers to those questions, our attitudes about human-ET contact will be forever transformed.

Although it may not be possible for all experiencers, some are able to share their memories of abduction/contact events with others who were there. Such sharing can be invaluable by creating a support system, providing evidence that the experiences actually happened, and helping to fill in memories of the events that individuals may not have been able to recall on their own. While human-ET friendships may or may not be real, the human friendships that can develop as a result of those experiences are.

"We don't meet anyone by chance."

Avijeet Das

12

Q: Do ETs heal humans and can humans heal ETs?

I have been privileged to be part of the natural healing arts community for many years, and during that time I have known many gifted healers who serve humanity not only with their professional skills, but also with knowledge and guidance provided by beneficent otherworldly beings. These beings have been called angels, saints, ascended masters and gods by the humans they have healed and guided, but today many people call them ETs.

The story of ETs healing humans on Earth is much more extensive than my own experience. Down through history, human beings have reported contact with otherworldly beings that resulted in the healing of a variety of physical illnesses and injuries. Sacred writings, myths and legends tell of highly advanced beings who bestow healing on specific individuals or groups, perhaps to impress upon them their power or as a reward for devotion or a sign of their favor. In those days, healing by advanced beings was rare enough to be called miraculous, but in modern times, reports of healings in connection with ET contact events have become so numerous that the phenomenon is now recognized as an accepted aspect of alien encounters. In fact, in the past few years, more individuals have reported experiencing alien healing than those who have reported alien abduction.

The FREE Study asked the question, *"Do you believe that any of these NHIs (non-human intelligence or ETs) have performed a medical healing on either you or another member of your family?"* Out of 1,368 responders, 50.66% responded *Yes*.

That data is consistent with the findings of UFO investigator and researcher Preston Dennett, who has reported more than 200 accounts of medical healings performed by ETs. In his book *UFO Healings: True Accounts of People Healed by Extraterrestrials,*[16] Dennett relates many cases of individuals who believe they were healed by close encounters with alien beings. These reports describe healings of injuries and dis-

---

[16] Dennett, Preston E., *UFO Healings: True Accounts of People Healed by Extraterrestrials*. Wild Flower Press. 1965.

eases varying from flesh wounds and minor illnesses and ailments to serious diseases, such as cancer. These healings are often effected by ETs aboard alien ships, but they are also reported happening in experiencers' homes and even in hospital rooms. In a hospital setting, the alien healer may appear as a human doctor or nurse who shows up in the room at night, performs a procedure that causes a cure or a remarkable improvement in the patient's condition and then departs. When the patient asks about the doctor or nurse the next day, they cannot be found, and the patient learns that no one fitting that description is employed in the hospital.

UFO investigator and researcher, Richard J. Boylan, Ph.D., co-author of *Close Extraterrestrial Encounters: Positive Encounters With Mysterious Visitors,*[17] has written:

> "*Healing procedures are sometimes performed aboard UFOs. While the technology used is often so exotic that the human subject cannot tell what is being done or explain the equipment used, a number of humans have reported ET cures of conditions previously diagnosed by earth doctors as needing attention. Treatments and cures have been reported for conditions like ovarian cysts, coronary valve disorder, vaginal yeast infection and obstructed nasal passage.*"

> "*Sometimes the results learned from the exam are communicated to the human, particularly if some worrisome condition is identified or if the human asks why a certain procedure was necessary. The purpose of the exam appears to be for the ETs to determine the subject's physical and genetic levels and their overall health status. Occasionally an ET will communicate to the human that a medical condition needs some attention and will indicate that either the human should consult an earth doctor about treating it or that it can and will be dealt with later.*"

Sometimes, healings appear to be purely accidental, when a person unexpectedly comes into contact with, or in close proximity to, an alien craft. A well-known case reported in 1965 concerned a police

---

[17] Boylan, Richard J. and Boylan, Lee K. *Close Extraterrestrial Encounters: Positive Experiences with Mysterious Visitors.* Wild Flower Press. 1994.

officer who experienced healing of a severely injured finger quite unexpectedly. While on patrol one night, he and his partner pursued a mysterious object in the sky, when the object suddenly turned around and flew over their car and a beam of light from the craft struck the car and illuminated it, including the officer's arm and finger which were hanging outside the car window. In a panic, the officers took off and lost sight of the UFO, but the next day, the injured officer noticed that his finger, which should have still been in serious condition, was nearly healed.

Another case of accidental healing by a UFO is recounted by a woman employed as a waitress at a truck stop in Mississippi. Her job required her to be on the road in the early morning hours, and one morning, on her way home from work around 2:00 a.m., a bright light hovered over her car and she blacked out. Suddenly, she awoke to find that it was 6:00 a.m. and she was in her car on the side of the road. Not knowing what had transpired, she drove home. But later, she had vague memories of being in a strange "examining room," with several figures standing around her while a "doctor" stood next to her and "passed some kind of rod" over her body again and again. She had suffered from severe arthritis in her knee, wrist and finger joints for several years; in fact, the condition was so bad that she was being forced into early retirement with no benefits because of it. But after the experience with the strange light, she discovered that her arthritis was gone, she no longer felt any pain, and she was able to continue working.

Many other cases can be found in the literature about individuals who experienced physical healings as a result of being accidentally struck by beams of light from UFOs.

Other, even stranger reports have been made about hospitals or clinics that have appeared in deserted or out-of-the-way places where people have found help or medical treatment in time of need. Often the treatment they received was very advanced and like nothing they had ever seen before, and the healing they received bordered on the miraculous. Strangely, however, when they searched for the place later, they couldn't remember the exact location and were unable to find it again.

Sometimes, healings are accomplished by alien healers in out-of-the-way places and in dire circumstances.

"ETs saved my life several years ago. I was driving home from college for the holidays on a winding mountain road, it was late and I fell asleep at the wheel and went off the road and down an embankment. I was thrown out of the car and knocked unconscious and when I woke up, I found myself lying on the ground, groggy and in shock, but there was a bright moon and I could see my car on its side a few feet away. As I was laying there, I noticed that what I had thought was the moon was now right above me and getting lower and I'm thinking what the hell, but I could feel warmth from it on my body. I thought I was either dead or hallucinating when I heard a very clear voice in my head saying "stand up." Well, I couldn't get up, but the voice came again and said "Stand up, it's time to go!" So I just scooted and dragged myself to the car and somehow managed to pull myself up leaning on the car. At that point I actually felt stronger and I took out my cell phone from my pocket, set the light on it to the SOS signal and then slid back down to the ground. Just a little later, I heard someone yelling from the road above. A family driving by had seen the SOS signal and stopped. I must have passed out at that point because the next thing I remember I was on a bed in their RV and headed to town. I had severe injuries, but I was alive and I owed them my life. Over time my body healed, but I had nightmares about the accident that got worse and eventually I had to go to a therapist for help. In hypnosis, I went back to the accident and saw what had happened, which blew me away. I saw the car go off the road, I saw my body on the ground and a large light emerge from the sky, slowly and silently lower and project a circle of light around me. I then saw strange, tall beings surrounding me who injected my body with some kind of energy, then told me to stand up, get out my cell phone and signal for help, which I did. I now know that I would have died if those beings, who I believe were ETs, had not saved me. I always felt that I had some kind of relationship with the stars before that, but since finding out what really happened that night, I've learned a lot more." TR

Many experiencers report being taken aboard alien craft where they are subjected to medical-type tests or experiments in which their bodies are pierced or cut open, but when they wake up later at home, their bodies are intact and there is no wound or trace of the radical procedures that took place only minutes or hours before. Some experiencers have reported instruments or tools being used on them that caused their incisions to knit without pain or scarring, so obviously, ETs are healing humans when they are finished with them. But are they doing so because they care about their subjects, or are they just putting them back together in order to hide their activities or so they can use them again in the future? Whatever their motivation, healing is being done.

ET medical teams (ETMTs)

Adrian Dvir was an Israeli computer engineer, author and medium who began working as a healer in 1994. In his book, *"X3: Healing Entities and Aliens,"* he explains how he assisted extraterrestrial medical teams composed of beings from various alien races. The aliens had been trained in human anatomy and physiology before coming to Earth, and brought advanced technology which they utilized to treat their human patients in an interdimensional clinic they set up in Dvir's home. The ET doctors were invisible to most of their human patients, so he was always present to provide support and communication between them. All procedures were done with the permission of the human patients and most procedures took place in the clinic, not aboard the alien craft. From 1994 until his death in 2004, Dvir assisted the ETMTs with many individuals who later testified to the effectiveness of the healing they received.

While the ETMTs that Adrian Dvir worked with were formal, organized teams of trained extraterrestrial beings, there are hundreds of recorded accounts of human healings by otherworldly beings that are less formal, but no less effective. Investigator Gordon Creighton relates the story of a young girl who received healing of terminal stomach cancer by a group of ETs who appeared out of nowhere.

"On October 25, 1957, a young Brazilian girl was dying of stomach cancer and was suffering greatly during the night. Seven members of the girl's family were present in the room when suddenly a beam of light appeared outside the house and the room filled with a vivid light.

Running to the window, her brother saw a large saucer-shaped object outside the window. A hatch opened in the side of the object and two small beings approximately "1.20 meters in height" with long yellowish-red hair down to their shoulders, and bright green, slanting "Chinese" eyes emerged. The family members watched, unable to move, as the beings approached the bed and laid out some type of instruments. One of the beings placed his hands on the forehead of the sick girl's father and began to communicate to him telepathically all the details of his daughter's illness. The other small being then shone onto the girl's stomach a "bluish-white light," which lit up the whole inside of her abdomen so that the family members could see the cancerous growth inside her. The operation to remove the tumor took about half an hour. Before leaving, the two beings informed the girl's father, telepathically, that she would need medicine for a while, and gave him a metallic-looking "hollow ball" containing 30 small white pellets and instructed him that she was to take one daily, which she did. In December of 1957, the girl's doctor verified that she was cured of cancer."[18]

If extraterrestrials do use their advanced technology to heal some humans, why don't they heal everyone? Perhaps they have special connections or relationships with the humans they choose to heal. Or maybe they don't want to draw attention to themselves by healing a lot of people. Maybe, despite their advanced technology, ETs are limited to the types of human illnesses and injuries they are able to heal. Or maybe their real reason for being here isn't about healing at all. The ET-MTs Adrian Dvir worked with told him that while they were happy to help individual humans, their true mission on Earth was to introduce themselves to all of humanity and convey the message that there are highly-developed races in the universe who wish to have contact with us. The healing work was merely their way of saying "Hello, we are here and we are interested in you."

Humans healing ETs

Healing between humans and ETs is not always a one-way street.

---

[18] Creighton, Gordon. *Healing From UFOs.* Flying Saucer Review, 15:21-22. 1999.

Some humans report that they heal ETs. Individuals involved in this type of work usually have training and experience in energy work, such as Reiki and hands-on healing, and may also have existing relationships with ET groups that have developed over many years before they are asked by the ETs to help them. This is not abduction. Instead, the human healers are asked for their help and are free to say no if they wish. It has long been thought that one of the reasons alien beings abduct humans and perform experiments on them is for the purpose of healing and invigorating their own weak and failing bodies. Whether that is true (and whether it has been successful or not) we don't know, but maybe some alien groups have decided to ask for our help instead of abducting us and taking what they want against our will.

Understandably, most people who are the beneficiaries of ET healing feel fortunate, and some have reported that after a healing event they not only possessed renewed health and vigor, they had healing abilities themselves. Some have reported a new interest in medicine, healthy living and the health of the planet that led them to pursue careers in those fields.

But not everyone has a positive attitude about ET healings, even when done for their benefit. Some people believe that whatever good work is done by ETs is not done out of kindness, but is really a front for dark, ulterior motives, and that one day there will be a reckoning when the aliens will return and demand some kind of payback for the energy and resources they have spent on us. At this point in time, that remains to be seen. But many individuals who have benefited from ET healings are grateful, and such healings remain one of the most fascinating aspects of human-ET contact.

*"The fact that some people have had their health
consistently maintained by extraterrestrials . . .
shows that they are actually practicing medicine
and are not just experimenting."*

Preston Dennett

13

Q: Is it possible to overcome bad trips?

Many experiencers describe their ET contact as blissful, uplifting and enjoyable - a really good trip. Others describe theirs as terrifying, painful and traumatic - a really bad trip. Dealing with ongoing alien contact can be a challenge and the challenge doesn't always end just because the contact ends. For some individuals, the bad trips go on and on in their minds even when they are no longer happening. Human minds are extremely impressionable, and memories that result from bad contact experiences can linger there and cause problems indefinitely.

So what can a person do to get over bad ET trips? Is it even possible? Human-ET contact events are as unique as the individuals who experience them, and there is no single method of getting over the bad ones. Even good trips can have profound repercussions that may be difficult to live with. Inevitably, each experiencer must deal with contact in his or her own way. Some may find therapy to be of benefit, some may rely on a spiritual faith or practice, some may find a foundation in supportive friends and loved ones, and some may get through the challenge by sheer strength of will on their own.

As humans, our beliefs and our world view are responsible for the way we face the challenges of life, including our ET contact experiences. There may be nothing we can do to stop bad trips, but we can change the way they affect our lives by changing our beliefs about them. I know that can be a tall order, because beliefs and world views that have developed over a lifetime can be very difficult to change. But if we want to make any kind of positive, meaningful change in our lives, regardless of what that change is about, the first step is to stop, think and develop a new perspective on the problem. I don't claim that it will be easy, but it can be done if there is a desire to do so.

Take a cue from Alcoholics Anonymous

Accept the things you cannot change, change the things you can, and have the wisdom to know the difference.[19] That's not just a mantra

---

[19] Based on *"The Serenity Prayer,"* by Reinhold Niebuhr.

for alcoholics and drug addicts; it's a perspective that has helped millions of people take control of problems in many areas of their lives and turn the bad parts around for good. And if it has worked for them, it can work for you - even with bad ET trips.

Accept the things you cannot change

If the bad trips have stopped, accept them as being over and done. Stop fighting the past and stop living in the past. Acceptance does not mean giving up and conceding that what the ETs did was right, but it does mean taking your personal power and stepping back from the situation long enough to figure out what your next step forward should be. As long as you're in your right mind and good sense, you have a foundation to stand on and plot your next move. Talk with friends or a counselor or therapist who can help you, then get on with your life and do the things that make you happy.

Change the things you can

If the bad trips are still happening and you want them to stop, you must first accept that they are real and are probably not going to stop unless you take meaningful action to make them stop. Then, you'll need to get together with a therapist, a friend or someone you can be honest with and trust, talk about what's happening and make a plan that you think will work and will keep you positive and energized, go over it until you know what you're going to do, and then do it. This will require work, it probably won't be easy, and you might not be successful at first, but don't give up. Your life is worth the effort.

Stop being a victim. Stop thinking with your gut and start thinking with your amazing, powerful mind. Change the rules of the game. Look at the situation without fear, analyze it and find a way to turn it to your advantage. ETs are interested in you because you have something they want. When they realize they can no longer get it from you on their terms, they will either leave you alone or your experiences with them will change. I know this is easier said than done, but in my many years of working with bad-trippers, I can assure you it's possible. Whether you are a victim or not is up to you. You can always change things if you are willing to try, and even though changes tend to happen gradually over time, every change adds up, and big shifts do sometimes happen all at once.

Q: Is it possible to overcome bad trips?

Have the wisdom to know the difference

You cannot change the past, but you create a new future every day. Worrying about the past and feeding off of negative past experiences will only get you more negative experiences. What's done is done, so as much as you can, let it go. You have the ability to change any experience from bad to good by changing your mind and then doing the work, but nobody can do it for you. Take care of your body with good health habits and take care of your mind by staying away from negative fear-based influences, wherever they come from. There are no quick fixes, and you'll need help, so look for positive, growth-minded experiencer support groups and knowledgeable therapists. But therapy and groups aren't right for everyone, so if you're okay on your own and you're making progress, keep up the good work!

And remember that ETs wouldn't be traveling to Earth from other planets or dimensions if humans weren't valuable to them. This makes you special. They need you. You are in a position of power! If you can come to accept that and learn to use it to your advantage, you can end your bad trips, or turn them into the best trips of all time!

Fortunately, most experiencers don't suffer serious physical or psychological issues as a result of their contact with otherworldly beings, but anyone who does should seek the help of medical professionals.

Life on Earth isn't easy for anyone, so don't hesitate to reach out for help if you need it. And if you ever get to the point where everything looks dark and hopeless, that's the time to get another perspective - and a good flashlight. You can do it! Good luck!

*"We cannot change the cards we are
dealt, just how we play the game."*

Randy Pausch

14

Q: Why do ETs visit at night?

Although contact with alien beings has been reported taking place at all hours, most abduction-type contact is reported taking place at night. Why? It may seem like a simple question with an obvious answer, but like most other aspects of the human-ET contact phenomenon, there is more to it than seems obvious.

Perhaps some ETs visit at night because they are nocturnal and their physiology prevents them from being active during daylight hours. That would make sense if their home environment is dark and they are unable to tolerate the light of an Earth day. It may also be easier for them to interact with humans at night when there is usually less activity in the environment to deal with.

Some researchers believe certain alien beings are active during the day, but because they exist in dimensions different from ours or because their bodies vibrate with frequencies that our human senses cannot perceive, we aren't aware of their activities. However, some experiencers and other sensitive individuals may be able to sense their presence.

But the most popular explanation is that ETs come and go under the cover of darkness to avoid detection. That also makes sense, except in scenarios where they arrive in large, low-flying, brightly-lit craft, in which case they either don't care if they are seen or they actually want to be - which opens up a whole other subject for discussion.

Although any of the aforementioned explanations may be correct, after years of studying abduction events and talking to hundreds of contactees and abductees, I am convinced that most human-ET contact of the abduction-type happens at night not merely because ETs want to remain out-of-sight, but because that is the optimum time for them to interact with us. And when it comes to interacting with humans, I think our extraterrestrial visitors know exactly what they are doing and the best time to do it.

Of course, skeptics and debunkers claim that reports of nocturnal human-ET contact can be attributed to sleep paralysis, nightmares or bouts of indigestion, and while those explanations probably do account for a certain percentage of reported contact events, they certainly don't account for all of them.

Brain activity

The human brain is composed of billions of cells that use electricity to communicate with each other, and the combination of all those neurons sending signals at the same time produces an enormous amount of electrical activity. When viewed on an encephalograph, this activity has a cyclic, wave-like nature. Simply, the faster your brainwaves are moving, the more mentally and physically alert you are.

Over the millennia that alien beings seem to have been in contact with humans on Earth, they must have developed a keen understanding of our mental processes and functions, and it's likely that they also possess technology capable of monitoring brainwaves and other brain functions to determine our level of waking or sleeping and the optimum time to interact with us, depending on their purposes.

Sleep state manipulation

When an individual falls asleep, his brainwave activity slows down from Beta (wide awake) to Delta (sleep) and then speeds back up to Beta upon waking. Ideally, the process should be smooth and gradual, but if it isn't, the awareness of sleeping and waking can sort of overlap and the mind can be awake while the body is still asleep. If this continues, a state of paralysis can occur in which he might be able to see and hear what's going on around him, but not be able to move or physically respond.

Sleep paralysis, or something like it, is also frequently reported as part of alien abduction experiences. Is this just a coincidence or are ETs using their knowledge of the human brain and sleep patterns to their advantage? The latter is a distinct possibility.

How might this work?

If whatever the ETs are planning requires their human subject to be unaware of what's happening and unable to resist, they might approach at night while she is sleeping and monitor her brainwaves until she reaches deep sleep, use their technology to keep her asleep, transport her body to their ship, perform whatever procedures they have planned and then return her to bed after they are done. When she wakes up, she might have a feeling that something happened to her or she might find physical evidence on her body, but she is unlikely to remember, because she was unconscious the whole time.

Alternatively, if they want her to be aware of what's going on but unable to resist, they might monitor her brainwaves until she is between waking and sleeping, hold her there in a state of paralysis until they're finished, then move her brainwave level to deep sleep and return her to bed. In this scenario, she is more likely to have some memory of the experience afterward.

ETs may also be capable of manipulating brainwave levels to induce sleep paralysis in their human subjects, to prevent them from struggling and harming themselves or their abductors during transport and procedures.

Sleep paralysis is a favorite Go-To of skeptics in their attempts to debunk ET contact experiences. Yes, sleep paralysis is experienced by many non-contactees, but that doesn't preclude the possibility that some individuals who experience it also experience contact with extraterrestrial beings. Nor does it deny the possibility that ETs may be capable of taking advantage of and manipulating the natural functions of the human mind, including brainwaves, sleep patterns and even sleep paralysis, in furtherance of their objectives.

Brainwave adjustment

Apparently, some ETs have the ability to make contact with certain humans by shifting their brainwaves to levels that are more amenable to communication. The book, *"Preparing for Contact: A Metamorphosis of Consciousness,"*[20] explains how communication between an alien and a human was accomplished by the human's brainwaves being shifted from Beta (wide awake consciousness) to the Theta (deep relaxation) level by a visiting ET. Further, the book adds that communication with humans is easier for certain ETs when a human's brainwaves are at the Alpha or Theta levels, regardless of whether the levels are attained naturally during sleep or purposely adjusted, because a fully awake human mind is too active and chaotic for ETs to connect with.

---

[20] Royal, Lyssa & Priest, Keith. *Preparing for Contact: A Metamorphosis of Consciousness.* Royal Priest Research. 1994.

Daylight contacts

Although UFO sightings and encounters during the day are relatively common, daylight abduction events are not. Perhaps if ETs want to physically abduct someone, they come at night in order to take advantage of darkness or human sleep patterns, but if they simply want to make contact, they do not require a nocturnal visit.

Events have been reported in which individuals have accidentally come across downed ET craft or hidden bases during the day and been taken inside, but such events are not typical.

We still have much to learn about why alien beings do what they do. But whether their modi operandi are based on daylight visits or manipulating our normal brain functions at night, after all the centuries they have apparently been interacting with us, they must know what they are doing and when to do it in order to accomplish their goals.

"I asked the tall one 'why don't you come during the day'? It said 'because you are unable to communicate with us when you are fully awake'. I realized then that my body was paralyzed and we were conversing telepathically." BL

15

Q: I have Rh-negative blood. Am I part ET?

Some people know their blood type and Rh factor and others don't, and the truth is that unless they have a rare type, it doesn't usually matter. But, interestingly, many experiencers report that they have Rh-negative blood, which some studies indicate is more common among experiencers than non-experiencers. If those studies are true, it could be mere coincidence, or it could indicate that the DNA of some modern humans was influenced by otherworldly beings at some point in the distant past, and possibly even that the beings who were responsible still retain an interest in the descendants of their human subjects.

Mainstream geneticists don't attribute the appearance of the Rh-negative factor in human blood to outside influences on our evolution, but at the same time, they are unable to pinpoint for certain when, why and how it came about, so they can't disprove it either. When it comes to a full understanding of the human saga, there are still large gaps in the narrative, and none bigger than the question of the Rh-negative factor and humans on Earth. There are differing theories in the UFO community and, in my opinion, the jury is still out. But it is a thought-provoking question, especially if you are Rh-negative.

Simply explained, Rh factor is a measure of a specific antigen in the blood - the D antigen - that stimulates the production of antibodies responsible for fighting foreign invaders, such as viruses and bacteria, in the body. The term comes from the Rhesus Macaque monkey because it's similar to an antigen that was found in their blood during early research into human blood transfusion reactions. You either have the antigen in your blood, meaning you are Rh-positive, or you don't, meaning you are Rh-negative.

Rh-positive

Most scientists believe that modern humans share a common ancestor with modern apes and for proof, they point to the results of blood analyses and comparative studies between the two. Approximately 85% of the modern human population has a blood factor in common with the Rhesus monkey - Rh-positive - so it's logical that all the humans in this group evolved from the same Earth primates with no outside interference.

Rh-negative

But what about the 15% of the population who are Rh-negative? Because Rh-positives share this trait with others, the Rh-positive bloodline can be mapped through human evolution, but the Rh-negative bloodline cannot. So, where does it come from?

Theories

Evolution is usually defined as a change in the characteristics of living organisms over generations. According to this theory, mutations in human DNA occurred gradually over millions of years as we evolved from apes to modern humans. Supposedly, such adaptations in our mental, physical and genetic structure came about in response to changes in the environment as humans migrated across the Earth. Mutations are common in nature, and evolutionists believe those responsible for producing the Rh-negative factor in humans occurred naturally, without outside influence.

Ancient Alien theorists examining the Rh-negative mystery think highly-advanced aliens came to Earth in ancient times and genetically altered native humans for specific purposes. According to them, the split that we now see between the Rh-negative and Rh-positive factors resulted from that manipulation. After some time, either because they lost interest in Earth or had other more pressing things to attend to, the aliens departed and left humanity to grow up over the ensuing millennia with their altered genetic thumbprint intact.

The *Creationist* theory posits that the Earth was created by a single all-powerful being who populated it with humans mentally, physically and genetically identical to himself and modern homo sapiens. According to this theory, evolution did not take place, humans have not changed since their creation, and Rh-negative and Rh-positive factors were created that way for some as yet undisclosed, divine purpose.

Mixing blood

Most Earth animals can breed with any other of their species without problems, but this is not true of humans. Rh-positive and

Rh-negative blood are not compatible and cannot be mixed in humans without serious consequences. Although most humans do not suffer ill effects from the Rh factor in their own blood, problems can occur in pregnancies where the mother is Rh-negative and the fetus is Rh-positive. Problems also occur in organ transplants and blood transfusions if an Rh-negative individual receives blood from an Rh-positive donor. Is this just a big screw-up on the part of Mother Nature or is it evidence of an effort by extraterrestrial beings or some other outside force to control breeding among certain races or groups of humans?

Mutation or intercession

Even geneticists who don't believe an outside force influenced the evolution of humanity admit they don't know for certain where the Rh-negative blood factor came from. We inherit the traits our ancestors possessed, so if humans and apes evolved from a common ancestor, which science claims is the case, their blood should have evolved the same way; but for some individuals, it didn't. Science postulates that the difference between the Rh-positive and Rh-negative factors was caused by a gene mutation. Mutations are simply changes in DNA that can result from many possible influences, and they aren't particularly rare, so it's plausible that the Rh-negative mutation occurred as a result of changes in environment, diet, disease patterns or other natural forces that haven't yet been pinpointed. But if it wasn't a natural mutation, then the trait must have been passed down from ancestors who were different from those who produced Rh-positives, or it must have been the result of manipulation by an outside force.

Why?

Studies in the UFO/ET field indicate that many experiencers are Rh-negative. Blood type and Rh factor are easily determined and run true through genetic lines, so perhaps whoever is responsible for the split in Rh factors had a specific purpose in mind. Some theories say the Rh-negative factor is a biological marker that identifies certain populations or groups of humans to be singled out by ETs for tracking or use in experiments, and the fact that many contactees are Rh-negative may support that.

Since the discovery of blood types and Rh factors over one hundred years ago, science has not made any significant progress in identifying where and how they originated or even in offering an explanation for their existence. While some experiencers report being taken by ETs for testing and experimentation which they believe is related to their blood type and Rh factor, there are probably more reasons than that. Perhaps in the future, geneticists will find the truth about the significance of the Rh factor in human evolution that will also lead to further understanding of its possible importance to our extraterrestrial visitors.

Much has been written and speculated on regarding the mysterious Rh-negative factor, and whether it is proof of alien intervention in human evolution is still unknown. But if you are Rh-negative and are also an experiencer, you may be able to count your ancestors among early humans who were touched by beings from the stars!

"So . . . is it then such a big leap to entertain the thought that some of us could potentially be of extraterrestrial or intergalactic origin?"

https://gostica.com/soul-science

16

Q: I think I might be a human-alien hybrid. How do I know?

A biological hybrid is the offspring of two plants or animals of different species or varieties. It happens a lot on Earth, on purpose and accidentally, with mixed (no pun intended) results. But has it ever happened on Earth involving otherworldly beings and humans? And is it still happening today?

Myths and legends of otherworldly beings breeding with humans have been handed down from ancient times and descriptions of such interactions can be found in the sagas and writings of cultures all around the world. Who were these mysterious beings? And what motivated them to mix their DNA with humanity's? They have been called gods, angels, demons and many other names by the humans they chose to mix with. But where did they come from, why did they come, and are they still here?

Human-alien interbreeding is vehemently denied by mainstream science and religion, but it has never been disproved. There are many individuals who say that while motives may have changed from ancient to modern times, offspring of ETs and humans are still being created and living on Earth today. The more individuals I meet who identify themselves as hybrids, the more I realize that, as with every other aspect of the human-ET contact phenomenon, this facet of the story is amazing and complex.

In their book, *Meet the Hybrids: The Lives and Missions of ET Ambassadors on Earth*,[21] Barbara Lamb and Miguel Mendonça introduce eight human-alien hybrid individuals who are living normal, active lives on Earth. These men and women describe their births, lives and families, and talk about why they are here and what it's like to be part human and part alien in the modern world. Although they have experienced similarities in their lives, they are unique individuals with different talents and abilities, likes and dislikes, and attitudes and opinions.

---

[21] Lamb, Barbara and Mendonça, Miguel. *Meet the Hybrids: The Lives and Missions of ET Ambassadors on Earth*. Amazon CreateSpace. 2015.

Families

Reportedly, different extraterrestrial races and groups may be involved in producing human-alien hybrids. Some can live and thrive on the Earth and some cannot. While most hybrids living on Earth have free will and do what they want, the different ET races or groups (often called families) typically do not interact with hybrids from other groups. This prevents interference with missions and protects hybrid individuals from possible manipulation by groups they are not related to and who they don't have an agreement or understanding with. However, it occasionally happens and when it does, it can result in a negative experience. One hybrid individual related to me that when she was a teenager, she was taken by an ET group that was not her own and, unlike the positive, loving contact she always had with her own ET family, this event was terrifying, violent and left her ill for several days afterward. Indeed, the experience was so traumatic that her conscious mind blocked the memory until it was recalled in a hypnotherapy session many years later.

How do human-alien hybrids happen?

Reportedly, both physical and spiritual hybridization processes are employed with human beings. They both produce physical beings who are capable of functioning on Earth, but they differ mainly in the way the hybrids begin life.

The most commonly reported physical process involves the abduction of human men and women for extraction of their sperm and ova to be combined with alien genetic material and implanted into the wombs of human women. Another procedure involves premature human-alien hybrid fetuses implanted into human wombs and allowed to gestate, but not usually to full term. At that point, the women are returned to the ship, where the fetuses are removed. Many experiencers recall seeing jars or tanks of strange-looking fetuses while aboard ships. In other procedures, human males and females willingly donate sperm or ova for use in hybridization programs, and mature human-alien hybrid individuals may choose to have their own children, utilizing various methods.

The spiritual hybridization process involves soul incarnation, which is similar to a walk-in, except that walk-ins always take place in adults and involve one human soul replacing another. In the spiritual hybridization process, an alien soul goes into a new human body at the point of conception, before there is a soul there. Usually, one of the parents is a hybrid or there is a close relationship between an alien family and Earth family who has agreed to bear, birth and raise a hybrid child. "Starseed" is a term often used to refer to this type of human-alien hybrid individual.

Many human-alien hybrids work, go to school and successfully participate in society, just like natural humans. At the same time, there are many hybrids who are not physically capable of surviving on Earth and must live their entire lives on the ships or in facilities where they were created. Experiencers sometimes report seeing and interacting with them in those locations.

In addition to hybridization programs conducted by otherworldly beings, there are reports of human-alien breeding programs directed jointly by humans and ETs in secret facilities on Earth. In some instances, hybrids created in such facilities or in related projects may be allowed to temporarily leave the confines of the facility for the purpose of determining how well they can handle life in a normal Earth environment. While people sometimes report encountering such individuals in public, most of them stay out-of-sight and keep a low profile or live in closed communities in remote locations around the world.

In their book, *"Raechels Eyes: The Strange But True Case of a Human-Alien Hybrid,"*[22] Helen Littrell and Jean Bilodeaux tell the story of a human-alien hybrid who was allowed to leave her support facility and live as a normal human for a short time. Although she was able to function fairly well in the Earth environment where she was placed, she was unable to consume human food, so everything she ate and drank was supplied to her by the facility. And because of her unusual appearance and sensitivity to sunlight, she had to wear dark glasses and a headscarf or a hat when she ventured outside her apartment during the day.

Why create human-alien hybrids?

Although Ufology has failed to devote much time and effort to

---

[22] Littrell, Helen and Bilodeaux, Jean. *Raechel's Eyes: The Strange But True Case of a Human-Alien Hybrid.* Wild Flower Press. 2005.

the aspect of the human-ET contact phenomenon that involves human-alien hybrids, individuals who believe they are hybrids have come forward to tell their stories and share their beliefs about why the creation of hybrids is continuing and why they are becoming more active among normal human beings at this time.

Liminal beings

In anthropology, the term "liminality" (from the Latin word "limen" meaning "a threshold") describes the quality of ambiguity or disorientation that occurs in the middle stage of a practice or ritual, when a participant no longer holds his previous form of being, but hasn't yet changed to the form he will hold when the ritual is complete. Some human-alien hybrids believe they represent this type of transition for humanity.

> *"The first time I was taken by ETs I was told that I am actually a human-alien hybrid created as part of a program to mix ET and human DNA to upgrade humanity to eventually be more advanced mentally and spiritually. As I understand it, I'm not the final version, but a step along the path so to speak. There are too many people on the Earth for ETs to change everyone, but groups of humans who have certain characteristics are having their DNA mixed with aliens and will reproduce and over time humanity will reach where it needs to be. Humans can definitely benefit from some upgrading and it makes me happy to know that I have a part in it."* TR

Characteristics of human-alien hybrids

Human-alien hybrids carry traits of both humans and aliens that express in different ways. Alien traits tend to be passive, while human traits are active, which is likely why so many modern human-alien hybrids look and behave like ordinary human beings. At the same time, human-alien hybrids may have anatomical and physiological traits that differ from members of their human family.

In addition to other things, many hybrid individuals have a blood type that cannot be explained by family genetics, their body temperature and blood pressure may be lower than the human norm, they may exhibit rare physical conditions or syndromes, have an unusual body odor, and they may possess unusual mental or psychic abilities and a proclivity to receive messages or downloads of information from otherworldly beings without symptoms of psychosis or other mental issues. They may also possess the ability to do energy healing on their own bodies and on others, in person and at a distance, and they may have a keen sense of danger for themselves and for people they are emotionally close to.

While human-alien hybrids are distinct individuals, there are certain things they report in common, such as growing up in unusual home situations and never feeling like they fit in with their family or social circle, feeling like they are always "on the outside looking in," having recurring lucid dreams in which they see themselves in alien bodies or locales, feeling a strong connection to "something out there" in space or among the stars, feeling from a very young age that they have a special mission, and experiencing repeated contact of various types with otherworldly beings throughout their lives. Of course, none of these is solid proof that someone is a human-alien hybrid, but taken together, they are strong indicators.

Missions

Many human-alien hybrids report that they are on Earth with a specific task or purpose. Such missions may include observing and relaying information back to their ET group about life on Earth, serving as subjects for study and experimentation or acting as messengers or liaisons between ETs and humans. The way they carry out their missions will, necessarily, be determined by the nature of their hybridization, the alien group they are related to, the mission itself and other considerations. So, as with many other aspects of the human-alien hybrid phenomenon, there is a great deal of variation.

While their contact encounters may not always be pleasant, hybrids are usually able to accept the difficulties and, in general, they have a more positive and less fearful attitude about contact and don't exhibit the problems that many human experiencers report. They nearly always report being born with preprogrammed knowledge, abilities, and gifts that guide their mission, enable them to accomplish their task and make their adjustment to life on Earth easier; although in many cases, they didn't really understand who they were and what was going on until they were adolescents or adults.

All human-alien hybrid individuals say that in their heart-of-hearts they always knew they were different and it was merely a matter of time before they realized who they were. I believe that if you are a hybrid, you probably already know or strongly suspect, and if you keep an open mind, you'll know for certain when the time is right. How you allow that knowledge to inform and affect your life is up to you. In the end, regardless of where we come from, it's what we do with our lives that really matters. Don't you agree?

"If we are to have any chance of understanding what is going on, we must listen to those who have been on the ships, interacted with the beings, or – as hybrids – are the beings themselves."

Miguel Mendonça

17

Q: If ETs are real, why don't they land on the White House lawn?

This is a favorite question of skeptics who seek to debunk the human-ET contact phenomenon. But whether you are a skeptic, a believer or somewhere in between, it's a valid question for which many people, including yours truly, would like an honest answer. If ETs are real and if they have been visiting us for so many centuries, when are they going to land on the White House lawn or in the parking lot at Joe's Bar & Grill or anywhere else and tell us what's going on?

The majority of our most well-respected scientific minds would answer that question with a resounding Never! According to them, while extraterrestrial beings may exist somewhere in the universe, they have never visited Earth and they are never going to, because the distances between planets and stars is too great and they are probably not technologically advanced enough to get here. Also, because we puny, backward humans have nothing to offer them, they won't waste their time and resources on us. After all, the White House may be a big deal to us, but it's not even a bump in the universe to them.

However, to the countless individuals who believe they have had contact with otherworldly beings, it's clear that they do have the technology to get here, they have been here for a long time and they are interested in much more than the White House. So why haven't they come out of the closet yet? Maybe because it's not the right time. Or maybe because they can do whatever they need to do without coming out. Or maybe for any number of other reasons they simply choose not to share with us.

But the real question is if ETs are visiting Earth and have good intentions toward humanity, why are they skulking around at night, abducting us out of our nice, warm beds and doing distasteful things to us. Instead, why don't they just step out into the open and tell us where they're from and why they're here? And while they're at it, we also want them to leave their ray guns and the scary guys with big bug-eyes inside the craft and send the non-threatening beings who look like us and speak our language - all our languages - out to speak to us.

That's what we really want. After all, the ability to accept individuals who look and act differently from us has never been one of humanity's strongest suits.

But all kidding aside, there is nearly incontrovertible evidence that ETs have been visiting Earth since before recorded history. Some have interacted with humans openly and some have stayed in the shadows out of fear or necessity. Since the dawn of human civilization, myth and legend have laid the groundwork for the epic story of visitors from the stars, and graphic representations of strange, otherworldly beings and craft have carried that story forward on cave and cathedral walls around the world. Despite our technological inferiority, it appears that ETs have been interested in human beings for a long time and they still are.

In modern times, individuals from all walks of life and strata of society have testified to the complicity of certain members of world governments with ETs in an exchange of information about Earth and its people for alien technology. While the truth of those stories may be dubious and the details sketchy, they are yet another pointer to the evidence of ET presence on Earth beyond mere lights in the sky and tales told around ancient campfires.

So the question remains, if ETs have been hanging around Earth for all this time and are so deeply involved with humanity, why haven't they come out of the shadows and shown themselves on the 6:00 o'clock news? Probably the most popular notion among Ufologists is that ETs will not make themselves known in public until humanity is ready to greet them without hostility. When will that be? Considering our propensity to regard anything and anyone we don't know with distrust, it probably won't be anytime soon. But if the time ever comes when humanity is truly united in peace, then all it may require is a heartfelt invitation.

Interestingly, in July and August of 1952, unidentified flying objects were seen and tracked over the Capitol Building in Washington, D.C., and more sightings took place in other D.C. locations in 2002. Some researchers claim the objects seen over the nation's capital at that time weren't actually extraterrestrial, but instead had been back-engineered from alien craft by Nazi scientists during WW II in bases located under the Antarctic ice cap. If they are correct, that may explain why no landings took place in Washington at that time. But it is proof that ETs have been in contact with humans at least for all of modern history, and doesn't preclude the possibility of genuine alien craft visiting the area.

The Old Testament of the Bible tells the story of the Jewish people who, after being delivered from slavery in Egypt, wandered in the wilderness for forty years in search of the Promised Land. How could a group of intelligent people wander around in such a small geographic area for so long without finding their destination? And why would a compassionate God deliver his people from the horrors of slavery and then allow them to remain homeless for so long? Although recent scholarship has cast doubt on the Biblical account, the traditional story goes that the Almighty was angry with his people for disobeying his commandments and punished them by making them walk around in circles for four decades. But perhaps their long sojourn in the wilderness actually had a practical purpose. Forty years was long enough for the older generation, many of whom had known only bondage in Egypt, to die off and leave behind a younger, stronger generation born in freedom on the journey, to build a new nation. That sounds like the reasoning of a wise and compassionate God who wanted his people to succeed.

What if the ETs have a similar plan for Earth? What if they are biding their time until a generation of humans arises that is ready for their arrival? Our children and grandchildren already accept the existence of beings from other worlds more easily than most of us. So maybe one day, when we older folks have passed away, ETs will land on the White House lawn or in the parking lot at Joe's Bar & Grill, and our great, great grandchildren will say, without fear, "Welcome! What took you so long?"

"Why haven't we heard from aliens? It's because they're already here. You just don't know where to look, do you?"

Anthony T. Hincks

18

Q: Do ETs have a sense of humor?

Contact with ETs is often a profound and life-changing experience. There is no way an individual can know how he or she will react until it happens to them, and even after a contact event, it may take weeks, months or even years for a person to fully understand and come to grips with what happened and how to deal with it. The human-ET contact phenomenon is vast and multifaceted, and while some contact events are unpleasant, many are joyous, and some are actually funny. According to some experiencers, ETs aren't perfect, they make mistakes and some even have a sense of humor, albeit not exactly like ours.

We don't usually hear about alien boo-boos and humorous contact events because the frightening and sensational stories are the ones that get all the attention, but whimsical contact experiences do happen. Whether extraterrestrial beings actually have a sense of humor is a mystery, but human beings certainly do, and knowing our sense of humor, it's not surprising that it would find its way into our ET contact experiences. Here are some remarkable, and funny, encounters of a different kind.

Who says ETs don't have a sense of humor?

"In my lifetime I've had a lot of trips with ETs on their ships and some of them have been positive and some pretty scary. But I remember one time they took me and I was on one of their examining tables and they had finished whatever they were doing and I sat up and hung my legs over the side of the table, but when I put my feet down toward the floor I guess I was a little light-headed and I slipped off the edge of the table and landed on my butt on the hard floor. It made a big splat sound and I farted and the grays standing around were startled and they all turned to look at me. I was so embarrassed and I started laughing and I know grays aren't supposed to have emotions, but I swear I could hear them laughing too in my head. Then I blacked out and the next thing I remembered it was morning and I was home in bed. I got

up and checked myself out in the mirror and I had a big bruise on my butt where I had hit the floor on the ship and even though it was sore I started laughing all over again thinking about it." AW

Wrong planet

"ETs usually seem serious, but I can tell you that they have a sense of humor or at least some of them do. One of the things they used to do with me on the ships is show the planets in our solar system and others on a big viewing screen and teach me about them. I was a science nerd in school and for a young kid I knew quite a bit about astronomy, and one time I was on one of the ships with a couple of older kids and the alien teacher was telling us about the planet Mars, but the big screen was showing Jupiter instead. There's a big difference between how Mars and Jupiter look. I looked at the kid standing next to me and we started snickering because the teacher was wrong. About that time another teacher came in, saw us laughing and saw the wrong planet on the screen and said something to the main teacher. We didn't know what was gonna happen, if we were gonna get in trouble for laughing or what, but then the words came very clearly into my head "Maybe we should let you teach the lesson from now on. Kidding." And we all had a good laugh." RS

Flying saucer circus

"ETs started taking me when I was pretty young. I don't remember the first time. When I was a kid the visits were usually fun because there would be other kids together in a big room with things to do and learn and tests given by teachers – sometimes grays and sometimes mantis beings. I remember one time when there was some kind of test going on that was scary and we were all upset and some of the younger kids were crying. Just then, the door burst open and there was a circus clown standing in the doorway! And then there was a dancing bear and jugglers and circus music in the room. There were trapeze ladies in tights and horses and we all started laughing and

dancing around and having fun. The bear picked up the gray teacher and started dancing around with her and from the look on her face, I don't think that was supposed to happen, but the rest of us just laughed and laughed. My contact with ETs since then hasn't always been happy but every time I see a picture of a clown, I remember that time." TR

Sinking UFO

UFO investigator and researcher, John Carpenter, investigated a case in Missouri in which a perfectly round, 30-ft. deep, 20-ft. diameter hole had been discovered near Jefferson City, Missouri, within walking distance of an abductee's home. The hole had been investigated by scientists from nearby Rolla, Missouri, using an arsenal of equipment, to no avail. Only when the abductee underwent hypnotherapy to recall the event, did the origin of the hole become clear. Here is what she recalled, in John's words:

"She had been recalling her abduction under hypnosis, remembering being led to the craft by an alien on each side of her. Suddenly, they let go of her and returned quickly to the craft. She bursts out laughing because she sees their ship sinking into the ground. Apparently, it had set down on top of a Missouri sinkhole; the weakened earth gave way - the craft sank out of sight. It was therapeutic for her because she knew that they were infallible and not so powerful after all. Besides, they dropped her and left quickly! The unusual hole remained as proof that something large, heavy, and perfectly round had been there overnight."[23]

Missing truck

John also reported this incident of an ET mistake - or was it another example of ET humor?

"One evening an Arkansas rancher was talking on his truck's citizen band radio to his wife back at the house

---

[23] Carpenter, John S., MSW, LCSW. www.alienjigsaw.com/et-contact/Carpenter-Abductions-Alien-Mistakes-Humorous-Evidence.html.

when he told her he saw a brilliant light coming at him from the pasture in front of his truck. Then the signal crackled and was lost. In the dark, she and others went out looking and found the tire tracks in the dewy grass stop dead without any trace of the truck or driver. Minutes later, the CB radio crackled on again with the driver reporting confusion and disorientation. They located him but his truck was on top of a ridge on the other side of the valley, where no road existed and with no tire tracks in the dewy grass leading to the vehicle. It was as if the truck had been neatly set down - but on the wrong ridge! If one is not careful, I suppose, many Arkansas ridges may look like another from the air." [24]

Do ETs have a sense of humor or, for that matter, any emotions at all? Or do they merely have the ability to reflect our emotions back to us? Or like the android Data, from the Star Trek television series, do the ETs who interact with us want to learn what it means to be human by trying out our emotions? I'm not sure, but I believe they are probably curious about that special part of human beings that is our sense of humor.

"Wisdom of the Ages: Do the aliens on the moon pull down their pants and 'earth' their friends for fun?"

Matthew D. Heines

---

[24] Ibid.

19

Q: What is it like to be an experiencer?

As I have said before, no one comes away from contact with alien beings unchanged. Regardless of their age, the circumstances of contact and whether the contact is positive or negative, once a human being comes into contact with ETs, he or she is never the same. Whether positive or negative, contacts with extraterrestrial beings are not everyday run-of-the-mill occurrences, and they challenge many of the biases and beliefs about ourselves that all humans share.

Cultural/social bias

Contact events challenge shared cultural and social knowledge. According to accepted norms, contact with extraterrestrial beings is impossible, so experiencers often find themselves either trying to deny the experience or suffering alone in silence, unable to reach out to anyone else for help in understanding what happened and how to deal with it. Understandably, most experiencers are reluctant to come out and talk openly about their ET contact due to the very real possibility of ridicule, loss of respect, increased stress between family and friends, and even loss of employment. Additionally, by talking about such an experience, an individual is relinquishing an important coping mechanism - the ability to pretend that such an event never occurred. Once it's out in the open and other people know about it, he may feel that he has further lost control of his life and is even more vulnerable. Worse, in some countries, even today, individuals are institutionalized for professing contact with otherworldly beings.

The challenge to our sense of predominance

The very thought of contact with beings so technologically superior to us challenges our understanding of reality and our place in the universe. Can ETs really cross vast expanses of space, transport us through walls, travel through time and do all the other things they reportedly do? After all the years they have supposedly been on Earth and all the history of contact with us, we still don't have answers about who they are and why they are here. If they really do exist and are as powerful as they appear to be, it's obvious that humanity doesn't hold the position of predominance and mastery in the universe we like to think we do, and that's not something our governments are eager to admit.

The challenge to our sense of safety

Probably the most difficult thing about being an experiencer is the threat it represents to an individual's personal sense of safety and control. Abductees often recount being treated like we treat animals, by beings with vastly superior technology and unknown motives. "You're being controlled by creatures who show no regard for your wishes or needs, without knowing what they're gonna to do to you. You're help-less."

Contact, especially abduction-type contact, can bring us face-to-face with the pain and fear of our worst nightmares. Even positive contact experiences often contain elements of fear, and many long-time contactees report that even though their contact events may have become more positive over time, their early experiences were threatening and traumatic.

Experienced anomalous trauma

The thoughts and behaviors of experiencers often fit into a pattern of responses to traumatic events that are beyond society's current explanation of normal human experiences and that it has no logical explanation for. Contact with alien beings isn't part of the normal human experience, and yet abductees/contactees may suffer very real trauma as a result.

Initially, before such individuals have had a chance to talk about their experiences, they often suffer from symptoms similar to those of post-traumatic stress disorder (PTSD). They may exhibit phobic avoidance of anything linked to the contact experience, they may experience intrusive thoughts and emotions or they may have nightmares, flashes of images related to the event and have trouble focusing on daily tasks. In addition, they may avoid the location of the event, written and video material about UFOs or ETs, and doctor or dentist visits that involve bright lights or examination scenarios. Some also report a decreased interest in physical intimacy due to feelings of vulnerability they didn't feel before the contact experience.

The next response to contact is often fear and anger, especially if abductions/contacts continue. This can be a difficult stage to move past and, unfortunately, many people get caught up at this point and spend years viewing themselves as victims. However, after speaking to an investigator or therapist about their experiences, even if no formal therapy is involved, many acute PTSD-like symptoms can begin to fade. After a while, experiencers may become interested in learning all they can about UFOs and ETs, perhaps in an effort to make sense of what happened to them and in anticipation of preventing future contact events. From then on, how they choose to go forward, whether to continue learning more about their experience or to put it aside and get on with their lives, is up to each individual, and people do choose to handle things differently.

There is more information on the symptomatology of PTSD as it relates to alien abduction and extraterrestrial contact experiences in the Appendix section of this book.

Fantasy proneness

The whole human-ET contact phenomenon seems fantastic, so it's easy to believe that experiencers must not possess the ability to distinguish reality from fantasy. But the truth is that there is no good, hard evidence that experiencers are more fantasy prone than the rest of the general population.

In their firsthand study of abduction experiencers, Sandra C. Wilson and Theodore X. Barber[25] found that levels of fantasy proneness, as measured by the Inventory of Childhood Memories and Imaginings (ICMI), a validated measure of fantasy proneness, were no higher than fantasy proneness levels in the general public.

From Spanos, et al.'s 1993 study, 40% of intense UFO experiences (involving seeing a UFO close-up, contact with aliens, missing time or abduction) showed average fantasy proneness scores when compared to a community sample.

When comparing the characteristics of fantasy proneness in UFO

[25] Wilson, Sandra. C. & Barber, Theodore, X., *The fantasy prone personality: Implications for understanding imagery, hypnosis, and parapsychological phenomena. In Imagery: Current Theory, Research and Application* (pp. 340-390), A.A. Sheikh (editor). Wiley. 1983.

contactees and non-UFO control groups, Kenneth Ring[26] found no difference. He concluded:

> "*Fantasy proneness is definitely not a trait
> that differentiates our experiential groups from the
> controls. Indeed, the average score on this measure
> is actually identical for the UFO groups. Accordingly,
> there is no evidence from our study that the UFOERs
> . . . are distinctively characterized by tendencies
> toward fantasy proneness.*"

Psychological effects

Some human beings experience traumatic contact events that
cause serious mental issues. The human mind has a reasonable ability
to block memories of events that are too traumatic to deal with in the
moment, but if such memories remain unremembered over time without being expressed and faced, they can cause problematic behaviors
such as phobias. Usually, these issues cannot be cleared up until the
contact event is dealt with.

D.H., a 32-year-old woman, came to me for help because she was
suffering from claustrophobia, an extreme, irrational fear of confined
places. She had been uncomfortable in closed spaces as long as she
could remember, without knowing why, but in the previous two years,
her discomfort had increased to the point where it was limiting her
ability to live a normal, active life. During therapy, this is what she recalled (summarized from my notes):

When she was around five years of age, her family lived in a ru-
ral area in Arkansas. Behind their house was a large field bordered by
trees. One night the family was sleeping, her parents in their bedroom
at the front of the house and she alone in the screened-in back porch,
when she awoke and reached for her doll. Not finding it, she got out
of bed to search and saw a bright light in the field behind the house.
Assuming it was her parents, she went out the back door and walked
toward the light. When she reached the back of the yard, she saw that
the light was a large round object with people moving in and out of

---

[26] Ring, Kenneth. *The Omega Project: Near Death Experiences, UFO Encounters and Mind at Large.* Morrow/Harper Collins. 1992.

it. Suddenly, someone stepped in front of her, blocking her path. The being was very tall and its face looked "puffed up and squinty-eyed." Frightened, she turned and ran back to the house, but she couldn't get the back door open, so she crawled into a space under the back porch to hide. She could still see the beings moving in and out of the lighted object as she cried herself to sleep.

Sometime later, she awoke to sunlight and the sound of her father's voice calling her name. He pulled her out from under the porch and took her inside the house. She had a few scratches on her elbows and knees, but no other injuries. Her parents sternly, but lovingly, reprimanded her for leaving the house at night, but nothing more was said, and the incident was not mentioned again. She was never really comfortable in small spaces after that, but it wasn't an issue, and she didn't link that discomfort to the childhood incident. The problem didn't surface again until many years later, when it was triggered by events in her life and developed into full-fledged claustrophobia.

During therapy, she recalled the event from so many years before and identified the people she had seen in the back yard as alien beings. She came to understand that the traumatic contact she experienced at that time had stayed buried in her subconscious mind until recently. Remembering the contact event was the first step to eventually leaving the trauma and the phobia behind.

Certainly, not all phobias arise from ET contact, but the fact that some do isn't surprising, considering how powerful and traumatic such events can be.

Contact - positive or negative

Contact between a human being and an alien being is very personal. No human being can understand what the experience is like until they actually live it for themselves, and whether it's beautiful or terrifying, it's a part of their life that may eventually need to be dealt with. But being an experiencer can be a great opportunity for personal growth in a myriad of ways and can lead an individual to help others as well, if that's what they are called to do.

Many experiencers consider themselves blessed and wouldn't exchange their contact with extraterrestrial beings for anything. Some believe they have important roles to play in raising the consciousness of humanity and protecting the Earth, and are happily working toward those ends. Others are not. Being touched by ETs doesn't make a person a saint, a genius or better than any other human being, but it does give them something special. Whether that something is a gift or a curse differs with each experiencer.

If you are an experiencer and are okay with that, I congratulate you. There are still many who haven't arrived at that place. If you aren't sure, know that although others are happy to help, the path is yours alone to walk. Try to stay positive, patient with yourself, open-minded and open-hearted to who you think you are, and don't worry about who or what others think you should be.

> *"Extraterrestrial experiences are like air; at times you can't see it, let alone explain it, nor do you care if science can't clarify it. Yet in its absence you welcome it."*
>
> *Tina Marie Caouette*

20

Q: Who am I, really?

Everyone has a sense of self or personal identity, and our sense of self is perhaps the most valuable part of us. Psychologists define "sense of self" as the way a person thinks about himself and views his traits, beliefs and purpose in the world. Beyond the basic need for a sense of control, we are more deeply driven by our sense of self - of who we are - than any other part of ourselves. As Descartes said, "I think, therefore I am."

Our sense of self includes the roles we play in life and the attributes, behaviors and associations we consider most important about ourselves. For example, I am a therapist, a sister, a friend and more, and all those different aspects of myself come together to manifest the person I am. They give me confidence and a sense of security, help me create a life that is happy, rewarding and worthwhile, and establish my place within my family and society.

Sense of self is an essential element of human personality, and a strong sense of self creates confidence and an ability to move forward to meet life's challenges. It's the foundation that underpins our ability to function in an often difficult world and, when challenged, even the strongest among us can feel powerless. But a challenge to our sense of self may also make us feel more powerful by opening our eyes to new possibilities and expanding the boundaries or our lives. If an individual is ready, seeing himself as more than he thought he was can be a wonderful thing, and contact with otherworldly beings can sometimes be the perfect motivation.

> *"I'll never forget the day I learned who I really am and where I came from. I was resting on the couch in my living room on a clear winter day. It was a bit chilly in the room so I had put on sweatpants and sweatshirt with thick socks and pulled a light blanket over my body as I settled in for a nap. The weekend before I had experienced my first conscious contact with beings from another world - an experience that, over time, would answer a lot of questions and explain much of what I had felt my*

entire life. Recollections of that experience rolled around in my head as I began to drift into sleep. But just then, a clear perception came into my mind and I raised my head from the cushion and gazed down my outstretched body toward my feet. As if I had x-ray vision, I could clearly see through the blanket and thick socks and I could see my feet, only they didn't look like my feet. Instead of my wide size 6's, they were small and delicate with three toes on each, covered in light gray colored skin. I then allowed my x-ray vision to move up my legs, which I could see were skinny and spindly looking, also gray colored. On up to my pelvis and torso - slim with narrow hips and waistline and flat chest. At that point I lifted my hands and saw, through my thick sleeves, delicate, thin arms ending in small hands with three long slender fingers on each. I couldn't see my head and face but I could feel that they were different. It was all very clear. I knew I hadn't actually transformed but I was somehow seeing another me - another self. And then I heard a voice in my ears saying "This is who you really are. This is what you really look like." In the split-second that it took those words to go from my ears to my brain I felt a weight that I had carried my whole life drop from my shoulders. I felt relief and I thought, finally, I know why all my life I have felt like I never fit in, like I was part of this world but also part of somewhere else. It felt wonderful. It may be hard for others to understand, but to me it isn't strange at all. They are both me and both Me's are real." DO

Many experiencers talk about being taken aboard alien ships and given information about the Earth, the solar system and the galaxy, either telepathically or through some type of audio/visual technology. Often, the information is highly technical, far beyond the person's educational background or knowledge up to that time. Although they may not recall the details immediately after the experience, later they may notice an expanded interest in science, physics, astronomy or mathematics, and a greater ability to understand concepts that were difficult for them to grasp before the experience. Some individuals have even changed their careers to the sciences or medicine after experiencing contact.

Some experiencers believe they have been taken as part of programs in which otherworldly beings were studying the natural capacity of humans to learn and accept new concepts and ideas about many different things. Whatever the reason, people who have been through these programs report not only getting smarter, but gaining more confidence and an expanded sense of self, and they tend to say things like "I never knew there was so much inside me." "I believe I can do anything now." "I am more than I ever dreamed I was before."

Experiencers often recount that contact with alien beings has expanded the boundaries of their lives in many ways, sometimes helping them gain a new sense of purpose or regain a sense of purpose they thought was lost. That expanded sense of self may reveal itself through mental, spiritual or physical experiences.

A few human-alien hybrids have told me that before they were born on Earth, they agreed to allow the knowledge and memories of their ET families to be blocked so it would be easier to live as humans, but later in life, they were contacted again by their ET group and shown their true identities.

"I was born into a very close happy home and I was an only child, but I never felt isolated or alone. When I was 9 years old my parents were killed in an accident and my world collapsed. I went to live with an aunt and uncle who loved me and treated me like their own and gave me a warm, protective and supportive home. Unfortunately, that wasn't enough – the loss of my parents was so devastating that I sunk into a deep depression and began to withdraw from the world. I was confused and I could never make up my mind what I wanted to do or how I felt or even who I was. When I didn't get better in a few months my aunt and uncle took me to a doctor who diagnosed me with borderline personality disturbance and lack of self-identity caused by my parents' death and started me on medication and therapy. In the beginning I thought things would never change but I slowly started to feel better and get involved in things and even though I graduated school behind the rest of my class, I didn't care, I was just happy to feel alive again. From there I went to college and graduated, got a job, got married, and have

had a normal happy life. After what I had been through as a child I thought I knew myself pretty well, but when I was in my mid-30s I had another experience that rocked my world, but in a good way this time. While doing meditation one evening, I had a very strong psychic contact with an ET being that turned out to be the first of many and that eventually led me to discover my history as a human-alien hybrid. It has been an amazing continuing experience and I think I appreciate it more because of what I went through as a child losing my first identity but then finding another one years later. I am so glad I finally did." RV

I suspect that there are many people walking around on Earth today who are not "from around here," and who are not aware of who they truly are. At the same time, there are probably many individuals who know or strongly suspect that their sense of self is founded on more than human DNA, but who have chosen not to share that suspicion with anyone or even to pursue it further for themselves; and there's nothing wrong with that. Most people find that dealing with one life at a time is enough of a challenge, and if there is more inside them waiting to be found, it will still be there when they are ready to search it out.

So who are you, really? Human? ET? Hybrid? Not sure? It might sound corny, but in the long run, whoever you are may not really matter, as long as you are the best possible You.

> *"I am not pretty; I am not ugly. I am not true, and I am not false. I am just me - a reality, a conception, and not a misinterpretation."*
>
> *Debashish Mridha*

21

Q: How does ET contact change lives?

It has been said that humans are *spiritual* beings having *physical* experiences, meaning that we are not mere corporeal entities, but also conscious beings, or as some call us - souls. As human beings, all our life experiences, from the most mundane aspects of our daily routines to our most personal and sacred moments, involve our consciousness. A study of the human-ET aspect of Ufology reveals that while many contact experiences do involve physical connections between aliens and humans, there is more going on than that, as I'm sure all experiencers would agree.

Most of the time, we humans are so preoccupied with our physical lives that we overlook the more subtle parts of ourselves, but according to what many experiencers say, not all ETs ignore those parts of us. Some alien beings who connect with us seem to understand our deeper natures and may even take advantage of them. Many experiencers recount that during a contact event, their ET handler looked deeply into their eyes with a gaze that penetrated their mind, laying bare their deepest thoughts and feelings, even their souls. If ETs are able to touch humans that deeply, they know we are more than mere physical beings. Perhaps that's one of the things that draws them to us and how they are able to make such lasting impressions, good and bad, on the human lives they touch.

Even though some experiencers began contact with ETs as children, others may not have been introduced to it until later in life, but may have felt that they were different all their lives and never understood why. Regardless of when contacts start or when they are recalled, it's reasonable to expect that events as profound as ET contact will have lasting effects on the lives of the humans involved, and recent studies have found that to be true. Many experiencers don't talk about their extraterrestrial contact experiences, but if they did, I believe they would admit that their lives have been changed in some very important and unexpected ways.

Two comprehensive studies completed in the last decade, the FREE Study and the *Marden-Stoner Study on Commonalities Among UFO*

Abduction Experiencers,[27] reveal the profound and varied influence ET contact has had on many individuals involved with it. In both studies, experiencers report changes in themselves and their lives, ranging from physical to psychological, that they believe are direct results of contact with extraterrestrial beings. Notably, all the individuals who participated in the studies confirmed that they were never the same after contact. Similar findings were published by Dr. Kenneth Ring in his seminal work, *The Omega Project: Near Death Experiences, UFO Encounters and Mind at Large,*[28] in which he concluded that, in general, contact experiences with extraterrestrial beings "tend to initiate some profound alterations in one's personal values and belief systems."

Mental and psychic changes

Many experiencers report that after their contact began, they became more sensitive to other realities and their psychic abilities increased. They also believe their ability to learn increased and they became more able to absorb complex information, including mathematical and scientific data. Some say they became more empathic with others and began exhibiting precognitive (knowing events before they happened) abilities. In addition, some report that they experienced flashes of what they refer to as "Cosmic Consciousness," and their minds greatly expanded.

Physical and energetic changes

On a physical level, many experiencers say after contact with alien beings, they became aware of energy discharges from their bodies or electrical-type currents flowing through their bodies and noted that electrical devices would sometimes malfunction in their presence. As a result of contact, some experiencers say they developed specialized abilities like the ability to speak and write alien languages. Many recount that after contact, they began to feel energy in their hands and expressed a belief that they could heal others by touching them. They also believe they received healings throughout their own bodies and that their susceptibility to illness generally decreased.

---

[27] Marden, Kathleen & Stoner, Denise. *The Marden-Stoner Study on Commonalities Among UFO Abduction Experiencers.* 2011.

[28] Ring, Kenneth. *The Omega Project: Near Death Experiences, UFO Encounters and Mind at Large.* Morrow/Harper Collins. 1992.

Spiritual changes

After contact, some experiencers said there was an increase in their concern with spiritual matters, and their compassion for others, their ability to love others and their tolerance of others was greater. They also felt an increased appreciation for the ordinary things in life. Their insight into the problems of others, their concern with the welfare of planet Earth and with ecological matters, their understanding of what life is all about and their conviction that there is life after death was enhanced. In addition, many of the same experiencers reported that after contact with alien beings, there was a marked decrease in their concern with materials things, their interest in organized religion, their desire to become famous and their fear of death.

The FREE Study reported the following responses to a variety of questions about how individuals' lives had been changed by contact with otherworldly beings:

> *"My desire to help others has"* out of 1,396 responders, 51.36% replied, *"Strongly Increased."*

> *"My compassion for others has"* out of 1,389 responders, 54.43% replied, *"Strongly Increased."*

> *"My appreciation of the ordinary things of life has"* out of 1,395 responders, 51.61% replied, *"Strongly Increased."*

> *"My concern with the materials things of life has"* out of 1,387 responders, 35.54% replied, *"Strongly Decreased."*

> *"My concern with spiritual matters has"* out of 1,393 responders, 58.79% replied, *"Strongly Increased."*

> *"My interest in organized religion has"* out of 1,389 responders, 52.34% replied, *"Strongly Decreased."*

> *"My desire to achieve higher consciousness has"* out of 1,391 responders, 36.64% replied, *"Strongly Increased."*

"My competitive tendencies have" out of 1,386 responders, 34.70% replied, *"Strongly Decreased."*

"My concern for the welfare of planet Earth has" out of 1,386 responders, 61.90% said, *"Strongly Increased."*

"My understanding of what is life all about has" out of 1,377 responders, 53.45% replied, *"Strongly Increased."*

"My personal sense of purpose in life has" out of 1,381 responders, 46.05% replied, *"Strongly Increased."*

"My belief in a higher power has" out of 1,385 responders, 49.10% said, *"Strongly Increased."*

"I believe that I am a more spiritual person now than I was before my interest in UFO experiences." Out of 1,381 responders, 65.10% replied, *"Agree."*

"My sense that there is some inner meaning to life has" out of 1,388 responders, 53.46% replied, *"Strongly Increased."*

"My concern with ecological matters has" out of 1,385 responders, 49.03% replied, *"Strongly Increased."*

"My conviction that there is life after death has" out of 1,383 responders, 54.74% replied, *"Strongly Increased."*

"I believe that my UFO experiences were 'arranged' or 'designed' by a higher intelligence and that the ETs have a role in this." Out of 1,385 responders, 68.98% replied, *"Agree."*

"I believe that my UFO experiences occurred so as to awaken me to the existence of larger cosmic forces which are affecting our lives and that the ETs have a

role in this." Out of 1,385 responders, 71.84% replied, *"Agree."*

"In my opinion, the widespread occurrence of UFO experiences is part of a larger plan to promote the evolution of Consciousness on a species-wide scale." Out of 1,383 responders, 71.15% replied, *"Agree."*

"Evolutionary forces are already at work which will transform humanity at large into a more self-aware, spiritually sensitive species." Out of 1,376 responders, 72.38% replied, *"Agree."*

"I believe that there is a higher power guiding my life and that the ETs have a role in this." Out of 1,379 responders, 61.64% replied, *"Agree."*

"There are higher-order intelligences that have a concern with the welfare of our planet." Out of 1,388 responders, 86.24% replied, *"Agree."*

Positive or negative?

Interestingly, current research indicates that the majority of individuals who have ET contact and who choose to speak about it view their experiences as positive, with those who view their experiences as negative in the minority. However, if you look at ET contact events throughout history, the majority of reports in previous decades tended toward the negative, threatening variety. While some experiencers still do report negative contact, those reports now seem to be outweighed by the positive variety.

The FREE Study asked the question, *"Do you believe that ETs are mainly bad, malevolent, or evil?"* Of the individuals who responded, 91% said *No*. The final data revealed that only 5% of the experiencers viewed their contact as mainly negative. Interestingly, this research runs counter to negative images of aliens often presented in the media and entertainment.

So, what's going on? Are extraterrestrials changing the way they interact with us? Or are we developing a more positive and confident attitude toward them? Has contact with alien beings changed humanity or have we changed them? Have otherworldly beings interacting with us always been benevolent and have we simply been deceived by sources on Earth? We don't know. But we do know that ET contact has influenced human society and made profound changes in many individual human lives - sometimes good and sometimes not so good. If you have experienced changes in your life as a result of ET contact, you are certainly not alone.

"I personally find that true UFO stories are among the most profound of all human experiences. A very close encounter with a UFO can leave a person completely transformed."

Preston Dennett

22

Q: How can I communicate with ETs?

This question is arising more and more frequently from scientists, researchers and people in all walks of life who are convinced of the existence of extraterrestrial life and want to take the next step of communicating with who or whatever they are. Interestingly, even some experiencers who have been in touch with alien beings for years are now asking how they can initiate contact, rather than continuing to wait for ETs to come knocking on their doors. And yet, despite the growing interest, this may still be the most controversial of all the forbidden questions.

Why communicate with ETs?

Regardless of the many positive human-ET contact experiences we hear about, negative contact events are still reported, and the human-ET contact phenomenon remains a risky business with no guaranteed safe harbor in sight. So why would any intelligent, level-headed person want to risk initiating contact with alien beings?

Skeptics and non-believers can't imagine why anyone in their right mind would want to waste time trying to communicate with beings who (a) probably don't exist, (b) if they do exist, probably don't possess technology advanced enough to get here, and (c) if they do exist and are able to get here, will only be interested in destroying or enslaving humanity. The great scientists of our day have come out and said as much. In their view, the smart money is on keeping our mouths shut and maintaining a low profile to avoid attracting the attention of the more powerful, possibly hostile, residents of the galaxy. And they're not the only members of the human race who aren't exactly eager to reach out and touch ETs. Many experiencers who have suffered through negative, traumatic contact with alien beings cannot comprehend why anyone would willingly expose himself to such experiences.

But if you ask scientists, investigators and explorers in any field of endeavor why they venture outside their safe, warm laboratories and libraries into the vast, mysterious unknown, they will tell you they do it to satisfy their curiosity and expand the scope of human knowledge.

If you ask Ufologists and contact researchers why they want to talk to ETs, you'll get the same answers. Boundless curiosity and a thirst for knowledge are hallmarks of the human race.

Some researchers and experiencers believe that extraterrestrial beings are interacting with humans for purposes that are suspect, at best, and malicious, at worst. They take as their evidence the many testimonies of individuals who have been abducted and subjected to abusive treatment by alien beings whose interest in humans extends only as far as it serves their own agendas. Those individuals are not interested in learning how to communicate with ETs. Instead of opening the lines of communication, they want to keep them firmly and permanently closed.

At the same time, other people believe there is no such thing as negative human-ET contact and that genuine ETs do not abduct or harm humans. Based on information they claim to get from military, government and even certain ET sources, they believe negative ET contact events are really hoaxes perpetrated by human groups for political and militaristic purposes. Genuine ETs, they say, desire communication with humans purely for the benefit of both parties and are open to human efforts to connect with them.

Don't call us, we'll call you

In the past, communication between ETs and humans has been either non-existent or a one-way call. There have probably always been humans possessed of a natural ability to communicate with alien beings, but they are rare. Some contactees/abductees who experience multiple and on-going contact report that they can sense when ETs are nearby and contact is imminent, but they have no input regarding the upcoming contact event nor any means of preventing it if they don't want it to happen. Historically, humanity has been at the mercy of ET agendas, or at least that's what we thought.

But in the past decade, researchers and experiencers have realized that this "don't call us, we'll call you" routine isn't the only paradigm that exists in the realm of communication with beings from other worlds, and they have developed methods that are changing human-ET communication radically. When one party only talks and the other party only listens, there is no communication. But when both parties talk and listen, in turn, communication happens. It seems that once we reached out and began to create a level playing field with ETs, the game began to change. So how do we find that level playing field?

Nuts and bolts = only nuts and bolts

Sadly, after decades of formal, scientific investigation, Ufologists aren't any closer to a true understanding of the UFO/ET phenomenon and human-ET contact than when we began. Essentially, the nuts-and-bolts standard scientific paradigm we have embraced all these years has not yielded the answers we seek. The big questions - are ETs really here and if so, why, what are their intentions and when do they plan to disclose their presence - still remain unanswered. Historically, the organized UFO community has utilized scientific methods in an effort to provide undeniable physical proof of the existence of an extraterrestrial presence on Earth, while conscientiously avoiding the other aspect of the phenomenon where those methods don't work - the uncharted, unquantifiable realm of contact and consciousness. Until we figure out how to navigate that realm, each of us may possess bits of the puzzle, but the whole, unmitigated truth of the UFO/ET phenomenon will remain hidden.

Consciousness

Human-ET contact has taken many forms throughout history, and human beings have played varying roles in that grand drama. While, typically, we have been relegated to the position of unwitting and ineffectual objects of alien manipulation, we are now finding another role to play based on a deeper understanding of consciousness – both ours and theirs. Humans are conscious beings and, based on their behavior and interactions with us, it appears that some extraterrestrial beings are too. Forward-looking researchers and investigators believe it's time to expand our investigations into the realm of consciousness and a new approach to human-ET communication.

On March 22, 1996, Adrian Dvir received the following remarkable message from the alien medical team that he had been working with:

> *"Life - the development of complex biological systems that reproduce themselves - is the most wondrous occurrence in the universe. An additional, wondrous event occurring in the universe is the development of consciousness - that is, the conscious being."*

A reactive approach

Since the 1960s, mainstream Ufologists have utilized a formal system to describe and categorize UFO sightings created by Jacques Vallée,[29] based on an earlier system by J. Allen Hynek.[30] The system consists of letters and numbers from AN1 (anomalous behavior of an object) to CE5 (a close encounter with an object). While still the method most commonly used by UFO investigators, by its nature it is an observation system based on a paradigm of ET-initiated contact that relegates humans to the role of passive observer.

A proactive approach

Three decades after J. Allen Hynek and Jacques Vallée created their systems, Dr. Steven Greer[31] updated them to express a category of close encounters characterized not by passive observation, but by human-initiated communication. Based on overwhelming evidence of extraterrestrial presence on Earth, the CE-5 Initiative promotes a new paradigm, proposing that as contact between ETs and humans matures, the relationship will require a more proactive outreach by both humans and ETs, and asserts that instead of passively waiting, humans can actively reach out to other beings who desire communication.

A level playing field

Human-ET contact is not only a matter of physical action, but also a matter of consciousness. As conscious beings, all our thoughts and actions are informed by our consciousness, and that aspect of ourselves cannot be separated from our actions. So it is with everything we say and do, including our experiences with extraterrestrial beings. We may be radically different from them in most ways, but if the ETs who seek communication with humans are conscious beings like we are, then consciousness appears to be a level field upon which an exchange of ideas and information can take place.

---

[29] Jacques F. Vallée - venture capitalist, computer scientist, author, Ufologist and former astronomer, co-creator of the Scale of UFO Classification. www.jacquesvalle.net

[30] Josef Allen Hynek (1910-1986) - astronomer, professor and Ufologist, best known for his work on Project Blue Book and the Scale of UFO Classification.

[31] Steven Macon Greer, M.D. - retired medical doctor, Ufologist, founder of the Center for the Study of Extraterrestrial Intelligence (CSETI), the CE-5 Intiative and the Disclosure Project. www.disclosureproject.org.

"If we want to begin to function on [the extrater-restrials'] level, we have to begin to BE on their level . . . if a big part of their existence is in the realm of non-local mind - consciousness - then we have to begin to look at that."[32]

And even better, consciousness doesn't require constructing spaceships, learning how to navigate the galaxy or calculating how many peanut butter and jelly sandwiches it will take to get from Earth to Zeta Reticuli and back.

How to find the level playing field

The desired outcome or goal of any communication is under-standing. Whether we seek to communicate with ETs or the people next door, the process doesn't just magically happen - it requires initial and continuing effort. Some humans possess the ability to communi-cate with ETs and do it naturally, but the rest of us will probably need some help getting started and guidance along the way. Certain types of meditation, remote viewing and focused consciousness exercises have been found to be effective. If you want to give them a try, Steven Greer, Lyssa Royal-Holt[33] and other contact researchers provide protocols for use by individuals or groups.

Communication with ETs may not be easy, for a number of phys-ical, mental and technological reasons. It's a big universe, and even if we are able to bridge its vastness with the power of our magnificent minds, to achieve success will require concerted effort and a willing-ness to embrace a new way of thinking about ourselves, ETs and the act of communication itself. But it can be done, and is being done now by individuals and groups all around the world.

The bridge

Altered state and deep meditation protocols have been studied in human-initiated communication with otherworldly beings and higher consciousness research for some time. Unlike contact events in which ETs are in charge, this type of research highlights the importance of the human being's role and increases our understanding of the func-

---

[32] Steven M. Greer, M.D.

[33] Lyssa Royal-Holt - contact researcher, seminar leader, author. www.lyssaroyal.net.

tion of the human mind as a bridge in human-ET communication.

Meditation techniques such as Yoga Nidra and brainwave entrainment have proved helpful when practiced correctly and perfected. The CE-5 Initiative contact protocols place an emphasis on brainwaves in the process of human-initiated contact with ETs. One experiencer described her first, life-changing CE-5 contact experience like this:

> *"A few years ago I had my first real conscious communication with ETs. Until then I had no real memories of contact but I knew a lot about it and was open-minded about it. When it first happened I was doing a guided session with a group of people to see if we could communicate with ETs. It was the last meditation of the evening and I was in a deep focused state when I opened my eyes and saw a glowing being a few feet in front of me floating just above some nearby scrub bushes. It was morphing into and out of different shapes and colors sorta like a kaleidoscope and I watched it, trying to figure out what was happening. After what was probably just a couple of minutes, it sort of folded in on itself and disappeared. I didn't know what it was but I knew it wasn't just in my mind. No one else in the group mentioned seeing it, so I didn't say anything, but I knew something special had happened. The next day I described it to the group leader and he told me that most likely I had received a personal message from an extraterrestrial entity and that if I was open to it, there would probably be more. Within the next few weeks there were more things that happened and every time they did it was just as I was going into or coming out of either sleep or meditation. As I researched communication with ETs, I found that it was all happening at or near the same brain wave level, the Theta level. So now when I want to communicate with ETs or other beings, I take my consciousness to that level and it's almost like they're waiting there for me." FG*

All religious texts and stories tell of human beings who saw, spoke to and received messages and guidance from otherworldly beings through prayer, meditation, dreams and other altered states of consciousness. Obviously, consciousness is the bridge that has connected humans to other beings, including ETs, throughout human history, and can continue to do so.

Are there certain ETs we might not want to communicate with? Probably. Are there certain ETs who might not want to communicate with us? Most likely. Communication with beings from other worlds will require maturity, trust and yes, a measure of risk. Humanity as a whole isn't ready to take that risk yet, but some individuals are and others will be as time goes on.

We still have a long way to go to a full understanding of consciousness. But I think it's like driving a car - you don't need to fully understand how it works in order to use it, you just need to use it wisely.

"I don't believe that consciousness is generated by the brain. I believe that the brain is more of a receiver of consciousness."

Graham Hancock

23

Q: Who took me?

The human-ET contact/abduction story has been compared to a mystery inside a paradox, wrapped in an enigma, surrounded by a black hole, and I believe anyone who has spent as many years as I have staring down the maw of that black hole will agree. After decades of research and investigation, the only thing we know for certain is that there are still more questions than answers. And of all the questions, the one that seems to pique our curiosity most is this one.

While researchers and investigators tend to see this question from an academic perspective, ET contactees and abductees see it from a perspective that is intensely personal and, in some cases, quite literally life and death. Since before recorded history, experiencers have tried to understand the strange beings who were taking them and their motivations.

The Earth is populated by a vast array of plant and animal life, with humans currently occupying the top rung of the ladder. However, despite being the most technologically advanced species on the planet, we are still not advanced enough to pull off what appears to have been conceived of, organized and perpetrated, since before recorded time, by beings who are infinitely more advanced than we are. So when we start asking who is taking us, the list of possible suspects is somewhat limited.

Extraterrestrial beings

In entertainment and the media, alien contact looks something like this: it's late at night, a flying saucer hovers over a house, alien beings beam down into the resident's bedroom, paralyze him and float him out through an open window to the aforementioned flying saucer where he is surrounded by more aliens, probed with strange tools and then returned to his bed sometime before morning, with no memory of what happened to him.

If all contact experiences were like that, it would be easy to figure out who is taking us. But they're not. As I've said many times before, human-ET contact events are as varied as the human beings who experience them.

Several different races and types of beings from other planets or dimensions are purportedly in contact with humans on Earth. Estimates by some experiencers and researchers put the number from 87 to over 200. They look and behave differently from each other and, apparently, have different reasons for their presence and activities here. In the FREE Study, respondents described the following general types of NHI (non-human intelligence) they have had contact with on alien ships or in some other dimension or reality:

> 1st most frequently observed – Human Looking
> 2nd most frequently observed – Short Gray
> 3rd most frequently observed – Other (not described)
> 4th most frequently observed – Hybrid
> 5th most frequently observed – Insectoid/Mantid
> 6th most frequently observed – Reptilian

Much has been written about different types of ETs who have visited Earth, where they come from, their motivations and agendas, etc., and I have included brief descriptions of the most commonly reported types in the Appendix section of this book. If any of them seem familiar to you, it may be because you have had contact with them. If none of them is familiar, it's still possible that you have had contact with extraterrestrial beings, because there may be races or groups active on Earth that we are not aware of.

Hybrids

While I haven't received reports of human-alien hybrids organizing or conducting abductions or experimenting on humans, some experiencers have reported encountering hybrids working with extraterrestrials on Earth and in off-world facilities. In those types of events, it might be difficult to identify who is in charge, but the environment and activities taking place should eventually reveal if it's hybrids or other beings who are taking you.

Humans

Some experiencers believe they haven't been abducted by ETs at all, but by human beings under the control of other humans disguised as ETs who are part of military groups, and who may work with genuine alien beings. These types of events are generally known as "milabs" - military abductions. While still in the minority of reported contact events, milabs have been talked about for several years and are becoming better known as individuals subjected to them come forward to share their stories. Also, some of the individuals involved in actually perpetrating milabs are speaking out and writing about their complicity in the programs. Why would humans disguise themselves as alien beings and abduct other humans?

As a cover for the real thing

Certain sectors of Earth governments have recognized the reality of ET abductions for many years, while publicly denying their existence and keeping whatever information they have a secret from the lawful, functioning governments and the public. This is the ideal environment for milabs. When an individual or an organization wants to hide an activity, what better way to do so than to disguise the activity as something they claim doesn't exist and simply declare that anyone involved or related is suffering from bad dreams, an over-developed imagination or mental illness. To most people, the idea of government or military agents dressing up like alien beings and abducting private citizens is so outlandish that it makes genuine human-ET contact/abductions seem outlandish as well.

Active military milabs

Some experiencers have reported being subjected to milabs while they were serving in the armed forces, at a time when they were particularly vulnerable. In her book, *Facing The Shadow, Embracing The Light: A Journey of Spiritual Retrieval and Awakening*,[34] Niara Terela Isley relates how she and other military personnel were subjected to experiments conducted by military and civilian scientists and doctors in various locations on Earth, the Moon and in space. Some of these individuals also reported the presence of ETs who observed or participated in procedures and activities. Compared to descriptions of civilian milabs, the treatment of members of the military has reportedly been much more severe. Often, individuals who have experienced military abductions also have a history of prior genuine ET contact.

---

[34] Isley, Niara Terela. *Facing the Shadow, Embracing the Light: A Journey of Spiritual Renewal and Awakening*. Niara Terela Isley. 2003.

Alternatively, some investigators believe that milabs are not perpetrated by the military at all, but actually by covert intelligence management groups that merely utilize military or paramilitary personnel and facilities to abduct humans who have had previous contact with genuine ETs. Such groups may not actually be interested in their human subjects, but instead, their purpose may be to gather information about the ETs they have had past contact with, their planetary origins, motives and agendas, natural abilities, technologies, etc. Unfortunately, some experiencers have found themselves in the particularly difficult position of being taken by both ETs and milabs, and facing the prospect of the same happening to their children.

To sow distrust and fear

Another explanation for the existence of milabs may be to create fear and distrust between humans and ETs. If the human-ET contact phenomenon can be twisted into an "us against them" reason d'être, it can become a powerful tool in the hands of whoever creates and perpetuates the story. Whatever our political or philosophical bent, humanity would likely unite against an extraterrestrial threat, if one emerged, and despite what many people believe, there is no proof that all ETs have the highest good of humanity and Earth in mind. So such a threat, real or not, might be very convincing. And who would most of us trust - ETs or other humans?

How do I know if it was ETs or milabs?

While it may not always be easy or even possible, some experiencers say they can tell the difference between genuine extraterrestrial contact and milabs. Alien beings possess technology that is more advanced than anything currently existing on Earth, while abductions perpetrated by human agents often betray themselves by their lack of technological expertise, coordination and skill.

For instance, in genuine ET contact events, experiencers often report being lifted by no visible means of support and transported to ships or other locations via portals or some type of unearthly transport system. In milabs, subjects say they were lifted by hand onto hospital-type stretchers or gurneys and then transported to other locations via conventional motor vehicles or aircraft. Also, they report being given injections of powerful drugs to control them and prevent them from recognizing their abductors and surroundings.

Another difference that has been reported between ET abductions and milabs is that if an experiencer doesn't want to continue ET contact - even abductions - he or she may be able to stop them. While not all abductions are preventable, some ex-abductees do claim they have achieved it. And ET abductees don't usually report serious, ongoing physical illness or injuries resulting from contact.

On the other hand, all milabs reportedly render the subject powerless and unable to terminate participation. Also, many subjects of milabs describe physical pain, weakness and sickness for days or even weeks afterward, which ET abductees seldom report. Milab subjects in the armed forces have reported the loss of days or weeks of time and often permanent memory, vision or hearing loss or damage due to such activities.

Fake ETs

Some individuals believe that covert human government or political groups are utilizing ET technology to build programmable androids that look like extraterrestrial beings and using them to stage frightening, negative abduction-type events. Why would anyone want to do such a thing? If someone wanted to convince the public that extraterrestrial beings are dangerous and that the human race needs to prepare for a future war against them, such staged events might be a good way to do it.

Counterintelligence experts acknowledge that good disinformation must always contain some elements of the truth to make it effective, and experiencers who are used in this type of program may be given specific disinformation and made to believe that they have been in contact with genuine ETs so they will convey that belief to others. If this kind of program actually exists, it may be very convincing and difficult to distinguish from genuine contact.

Any experience of being taken against one's will can result in physical, mental and emotional injury. Certainly, negative contact events can cause trauma, but even positive contact may result in issues that can have long-lasting effects on an individual's mental and physical health and wellbeing. Whether the contacts are instigated by ETs, humans disguised as ETs or human-fabricated androids, individuals caught up in them may find their lives altered forever.

The honest truth is that you may never discover who took you, but if you are having problems as a result, please reach out to friends, a support group or a therapist for help in getting on with your life successfully, with or without the answer.

"The only thing that scares me more than space aliens is the idea that there aren't any space aliens. We can't be the best that creation has to offer."

Ellen DeGeneres

24

Q: Can I stop ETs from taking me?

This is one of the most often-asked questions regarding human-ET contact - can humans successfully resist being abducted by alien beings? Not surprisingly, individuals who report having positive contact don't usually ask this question, while many who have negative experiences, understandably, do. Considering the countless harrowing accounts of ET abductions, common sense dictates that anyone in their right mind would want to stop them, if at all possible. But here, as in nearly every other facet of the human-ET contact phenomenon, common sense doesn't necessarily apply. The decision to resist or not resist being taken by alien beings is personal and sometimes complicated.

With respect to this question, experiencers and researchers generally split into three groups: those who say Yes, you can stop ETs from taking you; No, you can't stop ETs from taking you; and Yes, you can stop ETs from taking you, but you shouldn't. The bases for their answers may surprise you.

Yes, you can stop ETs from taking you

Some individuals say Yes, you can successfully resist alien abductions and prevent future abductions. Many contact/abduction events occur at specific periods in individuals' lives and decrease in frequency over time on their own, but some experiencers have reported that their abductions didn't stop until they offered active resistance. After that, some people were free of alien contacts permanently, while others were free from them for a while, but eventually, the abductions resumed. Some report that their resistance was as easy as merely telling the ETs to leave them alone and not come back; but in most cases, more was required.

In her book, *How to Defend Yourself Against Alien Abduction*,[35] investigator Ann Druffel describes experiences reported by individuals who claim to have successfully resisted being taken by ETs. The resistance methods outlined include mental and physical struggles (mind-

---

[35] Druffel, Ann. *How to Defend Yourself Against Alien Abduction*. Three Rivers Press. 1990.

over-matter techniques), righteous anger (summoning the power of your inviolate rights), support from family members (strength in numbers), metaphysical methods (creating a personal shield) and other forms of resistance. Using these techniques, some abductees reported permanent freedom from contact and abductions, but others did not.

Because extraterrestrial contact frequently runs in families, some adult experiencers have not only sought methods of terminating abductions for themselves, but also for their children.

> "I have had contact with ETs and other beings most of my life, but when I got married and had my first child, they seemed to stop. My visits were usually positive, but I wasn't unhappy that they stopped coming. When my son was 6 or 7 years old, he said something about seeing Jo-Jos in his room at night. I thought they were just his imagination and when I asked what they did he said they told him stories and they didn't scare him, so I didn't worry about it until my younger son started seeing them too. He called them trolls and he said they didn't talk to him, they just hung around and played with his toys. I had heard that sometimes ET abductions run in families and I couldn't help but wonder if ETs were coming for my boys like they had done for me. My husband and I took turns sleeping in the boys room some nights and we even set up a camera in the room a couple times a week, but we never saw anything and during those times the boys said the beings went away. But I didn't want to take any chances so I put some religious statues in their rooms and every night before they went to bed for a long time I went into their rooms and prayed that they would leave and not return. After a while, the kids didn't mention them anymore and I think they just stopped coming." AW

Some individuals have reported that surrounding themselves in white light or calling out for the protection of angelic presences has kept them from being abducted by alien beings. But it may not be necessary to use formal methods to resist abduction. A few experiencers have reported instinctively striking out at an alien being with their fists, a baseball bat or something else that was handy, or grabbing it by an arm or leg and jerking it off balance. One person used a karate chop to the being's neck to disable it. Shouting out the name of God, Yahweh, Jesus, Saint Michael, saying The Lord's Prayer or even yelling out curses and telling them to "Get the hell outta here!" have also worked.

Interestingly, the website *eHow* states that you can prevent yourself from being taken by aliens if you "line your home in very dark window shades." Apparently, the reasoning is that if your windows are covered in dark window shades, the aliens hovering above your house at night will think there's no one at home and leave you alone. Two prominent UFO debunkers also claim that it's possible to stop ETs from taking you if you (1) stop eating pizza at night, and (2) stop smoking pot.

Other experiencers claim to have successfully utilized a variety of different techniques, but regardless of the method, most formal resistance techniques seem to require strong faith, confidence and concerted effort to be effective, so if you decide to try one, don't give up if it doesn't work right away. You may also want to find a therapist or counselor who can give you advice, or a spouse or friend who is understanding and supportive and will stand beside you in your endeavors.

No, you can't stop ETs from taking you

There are individuals who believe attempts to resist abduction by alien beings are ineffectual because such beings are so much more technologically advanced than humans and so bent on controlling us that it's impossible to stand against them. They also claim that attempting to do so is not only a waste of time and effort, it can actually make an abduction experience worse. Some experiencers report that during transport to ships or during procedures on ships, they were told by their ET handlers that they would not be harmed and there would be no pain if they didn't resist. But if they resisted anyway, they were hit by a wave of overwhelming pain or terror until they stopped resisting, at which point the pain and fear subsided. Going through something like that once or twice would be enough to convince anyone that resistance is futile and, understandably, people who have tried to resist and failed are usually the same people who don't believe resistance is possible.

Yes, you can stop ETs from taking you, but you shouldn't

Many experiencers believe that ETs are here to benefit humanity by educating us to the wonders of the universe and encouraging us to rise to the level of our higher natures in our relationships with each other and the Earth. They feel that we do ourselves and our world a disservice if we resist contact with ETs who are here to help us. Before offering resistance, they believe an experiencer should stop and think about how much they can learn from beings as highly advanced as extraterrestrials, and consider what they will be missing if they refuse contact. Other experiencers believe they are part of an exclusive group of humans chosen to lead humanity onto a higher plane of existence, and they don't want to pass up the opportunity of being part of such a profoundly positive transformation in humanity.

Some individuals report that even though their experiences started out being negative, they later became positive, uplifting and enjoyable. So based on that, an individual who is having negative contact may decide not to resist, but to persevere in the hope that their experiences will get better.

The good news

For many individuals, abduction events, even those that have continued for many years, eventually cease on their own, so that's something to hope for if you don't enjoy being taken. And keep in mind that if ETs are taking you, there is a reason why it's you they are interested in and not someone else. If you can discover the reason and figure out how to change it, you may be able to stop them for good – if that's what you really want.

"The abduction phenomenon seems to be a mixed bag, with benevolent entities intermingled with deceptive ones. No one at present has all the answers."

Ann Druffel

25

Q: Can ETs control my mind?

Human minds are pretty easily controlled - by media, societal mores, religion, emotional and physical drives, by substances we consume and are otherwise exposed to, and by other influences seen and unseen - so it's likely that beings with access to advanced technology would have no difficulty controlling our minds if they wanted to. ET mind control is one of the most fascinating aspects of contact and one that bears closer examination because of what it may reveal, not only about the abilities of alien beings, but also the susceptibilies of our own minds.

Investigator David Jacobs stated:

> "But on the most profound level, it means that an intelligence which is a controlling intelligence can see into our mind, so to speak, which would mean a total end to the privacy that we each have inside our heads right now. That that intelligence, which possesses a technology that is staggering, is bound to ultimately be in control."[36]

Is he correct? Although to my knowledge no one has come up with solid proof, there are strong indications that ETs can and do utilize technology, and possibly their natural abilities, to affect and control human minds.

Memory control

Our knowledge of the human-ET contact phenomenon is based on what experiencers remember and are willing to share about their personal experiences. Some individuals have conscious recall of contact events immediately after they happen, some may remember them after a period of time, and others may need help recalling what they can't on their own. An individual's ability or inability to remember something can be accounted for by the way their mind naturally stores and retrieves memories. However, inconsistencies in memory storage and re-

---

[36] Jacobs, David Michael - American historian and Associate Professor at Temple University known for research into Ufology.

call can be attributed to outside influences, and reports of mental manipulation by ETs during contact events are common enough to assume that ETs may be able to control or influence an experiencer's memories.

Why would ETs want to mess with someone's memory? Human beings are much more likely to repeat an unpleasant activity if we don't remember how unpleasant it was when we did it before. So it makes sense that if ETs want to take us again, they might block or erase memories of earlier contact events or alter them in some way to make them more pleasant. At the same time, it's true that traumatic events of any kind can alter, block or erase an individual's memory, so while ET mind control might be involved in some situations, it's certainly not responsible for all cases of specific memory loss, even in experiencers.

Technological mind control

Many experiencers report some sort of mind control technology being used on them during contact events. They describe having a helmet placed on their head or being touched on the head with a wand-type instrument that kept them calm and may have prevented them from recalling the event later. Or an implant of some type may have been placed in their head. Some human-alien hybrids say that before their human lives, they made agreements with their ET groups or families that they would complete specific missions which might require them to undergo stressful or painful tests or experiments. In return, certain technology would be used to heal their bodies and block or erase any unpleasant memories so they would be able to return to their human lives and continue their missions. Perhaps that same type of technology is also used on non-hybrid human subjects to prevent them from remembering contact events.

Another use of mind control technology reported by many individuals consists of tests in which a human subject stands in front of a view screen with a device on his head while words or images are transmitted telepathically into his mind. One person who participated in this type of exercise was told that his mind was being studied to see how easily it could be controlled.

Technologies of various types have also reportedly been used by ETs to teach experiencers a variety of advanced skills ranging from higher mathematics, astronomy and physics, to navigation, building and piloting alien ships.

Some experiencers recount a similar mind control technology being utilized to compel them to do certain things, such as attempting to breathe under water, performing sexual intercourse with other humans or aliens against their will, or consuming solids or liquids that had repugnant odors or flavors. Individuals who have had this type of experience often find that afterward, they cannot tolerate certain tastes or smells, and may be fearful of places or things they didn't fear before the experience.

Telepathic mind control

The most commonly reported form of communication between humans and ETs is non-verbal, mind-to-mind or telepathic. This communication can be received in the form of words, symbols or images, or a voice in the person's head they cannot ignore or silence. Experiencers report that communications are often repeated in different forms, and the individual may be required to respond both telepathically and verbally to ensure their understanding.

Apparently, certain ETs use visual probes to connect with human minds. In one such reported procedure, an alien gazes deeply into the eyes of the human subject, penetrating through the optic nerve to reach control centers in the brain and manipulate the individual's memory, emotions and behavior. In a human being, the optic nerve doesn't actually connect to the parts of the brain that govern those things, but people who have experienced this technique say that the being's gaze went through their eyes into their mind, and they felt as if their thoughts and memories were being scanned. Interestingly, one experiencer said that the near-crippling headaches he had suffered from for years stopped after an ET performed this type of deep probe on him.

Screen images

Screen images are commonly described as images or visions of people, animals or objects involved in ET contact events. They may be holographic or telepathic in nature or may involve living beings that are utilized to distract, manipulate or confuse. They are also reportedly used for studying human mental and emotional reactions and in teaching experiments and exercises.

Many screen images involve animals, and the type of animal may vary, depending on the response the aliens want to elicit. For instance, if they want their human subject to remain calm, non-threatening animals like rabbits and deer will be shown; but if they want to elicit a fear or action response, prey animals will be shown. Sometimes the choice of animals will be appropriate to the surroundings, but not always. Individuals have reported seeing images of wolves in their bedrooms or dozens of white rabbits on their lawns prior to contact experiences. Images of people are also sometimes shown - usually clowns, members of protective professions such as doctors, firemen or policemen, and in some instances, even images of the human subject's dead family members.

How do screen images work? We don't really know, but there are two likely possibilities. Through hypnosis, technology or telepathy, ETs may have the ability to project scenarios into a human subject's mind that aren't really happening or that are happening, but in a different way from how they appear. Such images may have a personal meaning to the subject or make no sense at all; confusion can be a very effective method of mind control. Perhaps aliens have been studying humans for so long that they know which images are pleasing and comforting to us and which are repulsive and frightening, and they choose the ones that serve their purpose at a specific time and place. There is much evidence to suggest that contact often runs in families, and if a group of ETs works with a single family over several generations, it may know the family well enough to be capable of creating the screen images and other methods of control that will have maximum effect.

The other possibility is that extraterrestrial technology doesn't actually create and project an image that a human subject sees, but instead, it pinpoints and stimulates specific areas in his brain, and his mind does the rest. This is true mind control and manipulation.

Whatever method is used, the ETs are in charge of the show and the technology is very convincing. But not all ET screen images are perfect; some do contain errors and inconsistencies, and experiencers sometimes pick up on those gaffes, realize that it's just a show and manage to break free of the control.

Screen memories

Unlike a screen image, a screen memory is a normal function of the human mind in which a memory of an innocuous event camouflages or screens the memory of a related traumatic event that a person's conscious mind doesn't want to remember. Simply put, if an event is too traumatic for an individual to face, then a related inoffensive event may be remembered instead.

Normally, screen memories are a harmless protective function of the mind, however, if they appear as part of a contact event, they may be the result of mental manipulation. This can cause problems if memories of a contact event start returning on their own and the individual's conscious mind isn't ready to acknowledge them. Pieces of the real memory and the screen memory may get mixed up together, creating confusion and serious issues. If an individual wants to explore his contact experiences through hypnosis, screen memories that are there to protect him can actually make the process more difficult, and that must be taken into account.

Hoax encounters - virtual reality

In his article, *"Mechanisms of Contact: Does UFO Intelligence 'Hoax' Encounters for Experiencers?"*,[37] Dr. Joseph Burkes explains alien interactions with human minds by proposing that UFO intelligences perpetrate hoaxes on experiencers through their ability to create illusions, which he categorizes into three types:

VE-1 Virtual Experience of the First Kind - 3D visual displays that are interpreted as actual physical objects.

VE-2 Virtual Experience of the Second Kind - a real-time, full-sensory illusion that is popularly known as "Virtual Reality," as portrayed in the science fiction film "The Matrix."

VE-3 Virtual Experience of the Third Kind - a technologically-induced false memory implanted into a UFO experiencer's mind and believed by that individual to be as real as any other memory produced by everyday physical or mental activities.

There is no doubt that alien beings who are interacting with hu-

---

[37] Burkes, Joseph, M.D. *Mechanisms of Contact: Does UFO Intelligence "Hoax" Encounters for Experiencers?* 2015, edited 2018.

mans on Earth possess technology far in advance of our own which they may utilize to create illusions that convincingly simulate the appearance of physical objects indistinguishable from the real things.

That doesn't mean all close encounters between humans and ETs are hoaxed illusions and that no physical ET craft or alien beings exist, but it does mean that some of them may be, and sightings of UFOs and close encounters that are witnessed worldwide may be the result of both illusions and physical events.

Protection from ET mind control

Is this possible? The human mind is capable of amazing feats, so when someone claims that he can naturally protect his mind from alien intrusion and control, I tend to believe him. But what about claims for the efficacy of artificial protection technology and devices?

Some people claim to have successfully screened their minds from ET control with headgear fashioned from aluminum foil or to have scrambled telepathic communication by donning helmets lined with certain other materials. One such material is VELOSTAT®, a packaging material made of a polymeric foil impregnated with carbon black to make it electrically conductive. Typically used for the protection of items or devices that are susceptible to damage from electrostatic discharge, it can be found in a wide variety of products and processes. Another material, LINQSTAT™, has also supposedly been found by some individuals to be effective in screening out ET contact. I haven't tried either of those and I'm not endorsing them, but at least one website claims that they have successfully prevented several types of aliens from controlling human minds and abducting them.

Investigators and whistleblowers from different segments of government and military have come forward over the past several years with testimonies of covert black projects employing aliens and alien technology to control human minds. This is really scary stuff which, if true, presents a great danger to human welfare and freedom that we all need to pay attention to. At the same time, many experiencers who are reportedly in contact with beneficent ETs, say those beings are not interested in controlling Earth or humanity. This dichotomy between the idea of evil ETs in league with black governments and helpful ETs working with experiencers to benefit humanity makes the effort to get to the truth of human-ET contact even more difficult, and may further increase fear and distrust of all human-ET contact.

The topic of mind control is one of the most mysterious and frightening aspects of the human-ET contact phenomenon. We humans are holistic beings - it's impossible to separate our body, mind and spirit - and whoever or whatever controls one part, may control the whole. If ETs do possess the ability and technology to manipulate us mentally during contact events, how can we be sure that control doesn't go further?

Like other facets of the contact story, there are more questions than answers, and we have to keep asking and searching. One very wise individual said the following. She may not be right, but let's hope she is.

"The reason they are here is to learn from us, and when they connect with our minds, they learn who we are. If we are good persons, they will learn from that. We can teach them how to understand honesty and love." RV

26

Q: Where did the time go?

Time is a paradox. We spend time, save time, waste time, make time, take our time, etc., but we can't buy time and put it on a shelf. Sometimes time is our friend, sometimes our enemy. It flies when we're having fun and drags when we're bored or doing something we don't want to do. It's malleable and ever-changing, depending on our perspective, and yet our physical lives are structured and bounded by our concept of time.

"Does time exist?" is a question that has been batted back and forth by scientists and philosophers for centuries. Many physicists believe that because time is a measurable, observable phenomenon, it does exist. Others believe that because it's intangible and changeable, it's merely a perception. Albert Einstein is credited with saying, "The only reason for time is so that everything doesn't happen at once." But whether it actually exists or not, the concept of time largely rules our lives, and when it appears to change in unexpected, inexplicable ways, the experience can be unsettling and frightening.

Due to the nature and function of our brains and the demands and stresses we put on them every day, it's not unusual for us to experience occasional glitches in perception that may manifest as distortions or fluctuations in time. These are sometimes referred to as missing or lost time, gained time and dilated time. In addition to those glitches in normal brain function, certain mental disorders can affect our perception of the normal concept of time and cause the same or similar effects. Interestingly, missing or lost time, gained time and dilated time are also often reported in human-ET contact events, adding to the mystery of the phenomenon and leading experiencers to doubt the veracity of those experiences.

Occasionally, everyone gets distracted in the middle of a task and loses track of time, but an episode of distorted time is something more. Individuals who experience it as part of ET contact often feel uncertain, not knowing what happened during the minutes or hours they can't account for, and fearful of it occurring again.

Temporal illusions

Psychology offers different explanations for why a person might experience episodes of distorted time: temporal illusions, various forms of amnesia, disassociation and personality disorders, etc. Temporal illusions are distortions in the perception of time in which a person may perceive time as slowing down, speeding up, stopping or running backward, or in which the temporal order of events is mixed. All can occur for various reasons, some benign and some worrisome.

An individual's perception of time can also be affected by emotions. For instance, a feeling of awe has the ability to expand one's perceptions of time availability. Research suggests that time seems to slow down for a person during dangerous or fearful events, such as a car accident, a robbery or when a person perceives a potential predator. Empathy - the perception of another person's emotions - can also change an individual's sense of time.

Consumption of alcohol and drugs can also affect a person's perception of time. Stimulants typically produce overestimates of time duration, whereas depressants and anesthetics produce underestimates of time duration.

Missing or lost time

Generally, this can be explained as a gap in your conscious memory in which you believe you were awake during a certain period of time, but you have no memory of it, and yet you may remember events immediately before and after it. The length of missing time associated with contact events can vary. The FREE Study asked the question, *"If you experienced any "missing time" in your experience, do you know how much time was missing?"* Out of 511 respondents:

> 76 replied - less than 5 minutes
> 374 replied - 1 to 3 hours
> 44 replied - from 1 to 4 days
> 17 replied - more than 3 days

People sometimes experience short periods of missing or lost time in their homes, such as waking up at night to go to the bathroom or get a drink of water, not noticing anything unusual in the process, but when they go back to bed, they see the clock and notice that thirty or forty minutes have passed, when it should have taken only half that long. Or during the day, preparing a meal in the kitchen, not noticing anything unusual, then suddenly having a feeling of "waking up" to find that whatever they were cooking is now burned because they didn't turn the stove off on time.

Or they may experience this "waking up" feeling, along with missing time, while driving, mowing the lawn or when engaged in other physical activities. These types of experiences usually involve short time periods and, in most cases, they can be attributed to distraction or normal mental glitches.

However, missing or lost time is also reported in many known human-ET contact or paranormal events, and the time periods can range from hours to days. In his book, *Fire in the Sky: The Walton Experience,*[38] Travis Walton tells of being taken onto what appeared to be an alien ship, interacting with unidentified beings and then being returned five days later to a different location. After his return, he didn't know how long he had been gone until his family told him, or what had transpired during that time until he recalled the experience under hypnosis sometime later. In this situation, there was proof that Travis had actually been gone for five days, but some abductees report being taken for many days at a time and then returned to their regular time line, sadly, with no proof.

Gained time

A common example of gained time is when an individual is driving somewhere, usually following a regular route and not noticing anything unusual but, despite maintaining a specific speed, they arrive at their destination before they should have. They may feel dizzy or disoriented when they arrive, but in most cases, there is nothing wrong with them. This effect has also been experienced by individuals in their home, when they look at a clock and notice the time, then look at the same clock again a short time later and find that it shows an earlier time than when they looked at it before. Usually, gained time involves only short periods of time and the effect is attributed to visual or mental errors or glitches, but it's also sometimes reported as part of ET contact events.

---

[38] Walton, Travis. *Fire In The Sky: The Walton Experience.* Marlow & Company. 1996.

Dilated time

The term "dilated" describes the effect of time slowing down. As we all know, time can appear to move more slowly when we are doing something we don't enjoy or waiting for something we want to happen. But in those situations, we know the experience is due to our own perception, not the actual distortion of time. However, experiencers sometimes do report a feeling of time slowing down when they are in close contact with ETs, UFOs on the ground or when they are aboard an ET craft. As with missing or lost time and gained time, memories of dilated time related to ET contact may be recoverable.

What does it feel like to lose or gain time? A few descriptions I have heard include: frustrating, terrifying, maddening and freaky. Some people say when they gain time, they feel normal and clear-headed after the experience, but after losing time, they feel fuzzy and disoriented. Some researchers believe time distortions may occur as a result of dimensional shifts of some kind or when an individual comes into close proximity with dimensional windows or portals. This might account not only for the time distortion, but also the physical symptoms felt by the individual.

Causes of temporal distortions

Some researchers believe that time operates on frequencies - rates of vibrations of waves - and that the human perception of time is a matter of judging its frequency. If this theory is true, when people experience time distortions, they may not be perceiving the frequency of time accurately, which could make time seem to stand still or move faster or slower for the experiencer. Since we know that all our experiences are shaped by our perceptions, this theory makes sense, and it could account for time distortions caused by outside influences, including contact with ETs, and explain why they are reported in so many contact events.

Some individuals believe that missing time can be caused by out-of-body experiences - involuntary states where the spirit or astral body of an individual leaves the body and travels outside the bounds of physical reality. Time distortions may also be experienced in the vicinity of natural power spots and energy vortices on the Earth, especially if an individual is sensitive to the geophysical make-up, magnetic energy and plate movements of the Earth. Close proximity to interspatial or interdimensional portals may cause people to perceive fluctuations or distortions in time. In such locations, individuals often also experience physical sensations such as dizziness, light-headedness or tingling throughout their bodies.

It may not always be possible to pinpoint the causes of time distortions, however, if they occur in conjunction with UFO sightings or ET close encounters, if the individual involved has had prior contact with UFOs or ETs, or if more than one person experiences a time distortion event together (which is rare, but which has been reported), it's reasonable to assume that the ET contact and the temporal distortion are connected.

Time is a mystery that has occupied the minds of philosophers, physicists and mystics down through history, and many different theories and questions remain. Distorted time effects can be attributed to mental function, both normal and abnormal, but an experience as powerful as contact with alien beings can also affect an individual's perception of time, just as it affects his perception of everything else.

Time and dimensional portals?

Some South American experiencers describe having contact with alien craft that hover overhead and send beams of light to the ground to form space-time energy bubbles called "xendras." The individuals watching then receive a telepathic message to enter the xendra, where they either communicate with beings from the craft there, or are transported to other dimensions or realities where they interact with them. While in those other dimensions or realities, individuals lose all sense of space and time and may believe they have been gone for many hours or even days, but upon returning to their friends, find they have been gone only a few minutes or hours.

How is this accomplished? Is the xendra an interdimensional portal and do the alien craft have technology that allows them to somehow slip between dimensions and carry human beings along with them? Is it possible that they may actually have the ability to create a different local state of space-time that is experienced by the human participants? Or is it merely human perception?

We all experience temporal distortions from time to time and, in most cases, they are nothing to be concerned about. But if they recur

149

and are problematic, they can be indications of serious medical or psychological problems that should be taken seriously and referred to a medical professional for diagnosis and treatment, if appropriate.

"Lost time is never found again."

Benjamin Franklin

27

Q: Why are animals part of contact events?

Animals play important roles in our lives in innumerable ways. They are our beloved pets and companions, they are an important part of the Earth environment, they serve us and we survive off them. So it's not surprising that they often play a role in human-ET contact as well.

Contact events may involve animals that an experiencer recognizes, wild animals that are part of his everyday environment or that he doesn't normally interact with, or fantastical animals that don't exist in his everyday reality. In many instances, these animals appear normal at first, but after a few minutes, the experiencer will begin to notice there is something unnatural or wrong about the animal, such as its size or behavior. Sometimes normal-appearing animals show up in unusual locations or in normal locations, but in greater-than-normal numbers, or shapeshifting and morphing in appearance. In nearly every case, something will be off about the animal or the situation, and frequently, they will be precursors to abduction or contact events.

One individual who has experienced multiple abductions/contacts recounts that immediately before each event, he sees a hologram-like symbol, "most often an owl," in his visual field which he believes is being projected by the beings who are going to take him. When that image appears, he understands that his contact experience will begin soon and that it's time to "prepare for school or to learn."[39]

Another experiencer relates an animal incident involving missing time and possible abduction. Upon returning home from a trip one evening, she was surprised to see several white rabbits lined up along the driveway to her house, which was unusual, because she didn't own white rabbits and, to her knowledge, neither did any of her neighbors. She pulled into the driveway, stopped the car and turned off the engine and, feeling dizzy, closed her eyes momentarily. When she opened them, the rabbits were gone. Intending to unload her bags from the

---

[39] Mack, John E. M.D. *Abduction: Human Encounters With Aliens.* Charles Scribner's Sons. 1994.

car and investigate further, she went into the house and noticed that it was nearly two hours later than when she had pulled into the driveway, and she couldn't remember anything during that time. In the next few days she asked her neighbors if any of them had seen the rabbits in her yard or anywhere else in the neighborhood, but no one knew what she was talking about. Since then, she has had other experiences involving white rabbits and missing time, but she doesn't understand their meaning.

John Mack and other investigators who interviewed many abductees and published their findings, found that contact with therianthropic aliens - strange humanoid beings that either had certain animal characteristics or were fully transformed into animals - were fairly common in the abduction and contact reports they had studied. "The aliens appear to be consummate shape-shifters," wrote Mack, "often appearing, initially, to the abductee as animals - owls, eagles, raccoons, and deer are among the creatures the abductees have seen initially."

> *"Peter's abduction began when a group of small beings appeared in his room and a beam of light lifted him off of his bed. As he floated out of the house and into the air, he got a close look at one of the beings. 'Its eyes', he said, were very dark and deeply set in its face, 'like an animal's eyes. Like a raccoon's eyes.'"* [40]

> *"Moments before her abduction by small humanoids, Virginia Horton remembered talking with an 'intelligent gray deer' and added 'there was a person inside the deer.'" She saw the same deer and communicated with it on subsequent occasions."* [41]

Another abductee reported seeing a deer looking at her through a window of her home just before she was taken. At the time, she lived in a big city where there were no deer or other large wildlife.

Investigator Nick Redfern tells the story of a woman abducted by aliens who found herself lying on a table aboard their ship. One of the aliens placed a box on her stomach and what looked like a large spider

---

[40] Ibid.

[41] Harpur, Patrick. *Daimonic Reality: A Field Guide to the Otherworld.* Pine Winds Press. 1994.

emerged from the box, crawled up her body and inserted one its legs into her right nostril. There was a flash of intense pain, a moment of blackness, and then she suddenly found herself back in her car from which she had been abducted hours earlier.

One abductee who David Jacobs interviewed saw a wolf in her bedroom one night prior to an abduction and described that the wolf was standing on the bed staring intently into her eyes. She clearly remembered its fur, fangs and eyes.[42]

Another individual interviewed by John Mack told about being taken by "scary owls with big eyes" to a "space ship" which he also described as "a big boat in the sky." The "owls floated down from the sky" to pick him up. On one occasion he said that "monster owls" had attacked him on the ship, hurting his toe.[43]

The author Whitley Strieber stated that he was confronted by the large, hypnotic eyes of a barn owl staring at him through the window of his home at the beginning of an abduction.

The abduction of a woman on the West Coast of the United States started when an entity that she described as a "five-foot tall owl" strode down the highway toward her parked jeep and stared at her over the hood.

Another individual reported that her experience began when a large owl swooped down from the sky and hovered close to her face. Its wings didn't seem to flap and its big, dark eyes filled "three-quarters of its head."[44]

One abductee reported that while aboard an alien craft, she emerged into a chamber that contained a huge tree with a lush canopy of leaves. On each branch of the tree there was a large nest of twigs, and in each nest, an eagle was sitting quietly and peacefully. Fascinated by the serene beauty of the birds, she strolled around the tree gazing up at them, but as she looked more closely, she realized the eagles weren't real animals, but actually human-alien hybrid fetuses being incubated

---

[42] Jacobs, David. *Secret Life: Firsthand, Documented Accounts of UFO Abductions.* Fireside. 1993.

[43] Mack, John E., M.D. *Passport to the Cosmos.* White Crow Books. 1999.

[44] Ibid.

in containers on the tree branches.

In another incident, a woman recalled when she was seven years of age seeing a fifteen-foot tall kangaroo in a public park that later morphed into a small spacecraft.

Categories of animal involvement

There are hundreds of reports of animal involvement in contact/ abduction events, but a review of reports, research and investigations into the subject reveal a few general categories in which animals are most often involved, and the possible reasons.

As screen images

Screen imagery is common during human-ET contact. When animals are utilized, they are often non-threatening animals, such as deer, rabbits or other small animals; however, birds of prey, like eagles and owls, are also common. The purpose is likely to distract or calm the abductee/contactee, or make them remember the unusual animal and think the whole experience was just a weird dream. However, experiencers who are more aware and retain memories of similar events may know better and recognize the image as part of a contact or abduction process.

Animals aboard alien craft

In their book, *Secret Vows: Our Lives With Extraterrestrials,*[45] researchers Bert and Denise Twiggs share their perspective about why some extraterrestrials are interested in Earth animals.

> *"We were shown to a room that I recognized immediately from my own memories. This room is a veterinary clinic. Animals that they have 'collected' from Earth are taken to this room before being brought into their society. If they locate an animal that has been injured to the point that it will not live and there are no humans in the area, they may take the animal with them and try to save it ... If the animal lives, it is worked with and taught to communicate, and if it is a natural animal of the wild, it*

---

[45] Twiggs, Denise Rieb & Twiggs, Bert. *Secret Vows: Our Lives With Extraterrestrials.* Wild Flower Press. 1992.

is put in the reserve, free to roam ... The domestic animals are given to families."

Some experiencers report that while aboard ET craft, they were allowed to walk freely and explore certain areas of the craft, including one of the areas where animals - sometimes very unusual animals - were kept. This area is often described as a large area filled with spacious glass rooms that sometimes have low backlighting so as not to disturb the animals. They have also been described as similar to the interior of a coliseum, but instead of seating for an audience, there are multiple levels of glass rooms where animals are kept.

Other descriptions are of large, open, natural-appearing environments with plants and soil. Native Earth animals have been seen in these environments and also what appear to be hybrids of Earth and alien animals. One experiencer described two large glass enclosures:

"One had two gorilla type beings inside with a large cat. The two hairy beings were sleeping. The cat appeared to be a domestic breed, but it was very large, weighing at least 50 pounds."

Another animal was described as a " ... half lion and half reptile ... lying on its back." Its mouth had fallen open as it slept and while looking at the animal's mouth, they could see, "rows and rows of teeth," similar to those of a shark.

ET manipulation of animals

Based on reports of some experiencers, there is also evidence that extraterrestrials may use animals or screen images of animals as psychological tools to learn about human emotions and motivations or to get their human subjects to do what they want. These may include (1) putting an animal in danger to see if the human will risk his or her life to save it, (2) making a human choose between the lives of other humans or animals, (3) making the subject watch animals die and not be allowed to help them, (4) cutting portions of a live animal's body in view of the human, or (5) abducting the human's own animals for a variety of reasons.

"Into The Fringe: A True Story of Alien Abduction,"[46] by Karla Turner, relates the regressive hypnosis session of an experiencer referred to as Fred. Under hypnosis, Fred describes a medical procedure in which his bodily fluids were placed into an animal, and he encounters another animal which he believes was part human.

> *"FRED: I feel like they are doing something to me with the animal . . . they are doing something with me, my blood, my sperm, and my genes. They are injecting my fluids into this animal. I think it's stupid, I don't like it. Why are they doing this?"*

> *"I think I was lying down, and they were doing something to the animal . . . taking something from me and putting it into the animal. Then I remember seeing another type of animal running around. I can't remember what the animal looked like, but it was bizarre. Seems like the animal is part human, part animal. Like a small child around two years old. The one animal that appears to be part human seems to be real hairy."*

Fred then continues to say that the beings in charge of the procedures were "Grays." He recalled that they took his semen and placed it into the vaginal area of the animal, which had hooves, like a cow, and he believes that,

> *"They are regenerating from animal to human, from human to animal. Regenerating DNA."*

Animal mutilation

Also known as bovine excision and unexplained livestock death, since 1973, thousands of cattle and other animals have been found dead in North America under mysterious circumstances, with all their blood and certain organs removed. Because of the hi-tech nature of the mutilations, reports of UFOs sighted at or near the locations and times of some of the events, and the fact that no evidence of human involvement has been found, extraterrestrial or interdimensional beings are generally blamed. I don't address the subject of animal mutilations ex-

---

[46] Turner, Karla, Ph.D. *Into the Fringe: A True Story of Alien Abduction.* Wordswithmeaning.org. 2014.

tensively here because they don't appear to directly involve human-ET abductions or collusion between humans and ETs, but it's not my intention to deny the importance of the subject by omission. The work of investigators and researchers has established its importance, and I believe it is still one of the most pertinent forbidden questions that needs to be answered.

In my experiencer therapy practice over the years, I have heard many stories of animals being involved in contact and abduction events in different ways. But I have also heard many stories of strange animal presences and behavior in which there were no other signs or memories of contact. Does that mean that an abduction or contact didn't occur or that it did occur and just wasn't remembered? Or is it possible that there can sometimes be other explanations that we just haven't yet realized?

"Five-foot tall owls and talking deer? In the realm of consciousness, the possibilities are inconceivable."

P. Gerard

28

Q: USOs?

On January 3, 1979, while driving with two of his friends along the coast near Hialeah, Florida, Filiberto Cardenas was picked up by a UFO. In one report of his story, he found himself in the presence of three strange figures, one of whom placed a helmet on his head and spoke to him in a language he didn't understand. Images were projected into his mind of scenes from the past, present and future of humankind, including predictions involving the succession of future popes, the 1980 election of President Ronald Reagan, the 1981 assassination of Egyptian President Anwar Sadat, the 1985 Mexico City earthquake, the 1989 student demonstration in Tiananmen Square and the 1990 Gulf War against Saddam Hussein. He was then taken to a smaller craft that disembarked from the main ship and plunged into the ocean below at an incredible rate of speed. After only a few seconds, the small craft entered an underwater tunnel on the ocean floor whose walls appeared smooth and were illuminated by an unseen power source. Shortly after, the craft emerged from the water in a large, dry cavern-like room where he was welcomed by a humanoid being who claimed to be from Earth, and who said he had been working with extraterrestrial beings for many years. Filiberto was then taken on a tour of an undersea base and city, and then returned safely to land, near his original abduction site.

While Cardenas' experience was similar in many respects to typical alien abduction scenarios, what made it different was his claim that it involved an alien craft that functioned both in the air and underwater - a USO, or unidentified submerged object. Many USOs have been observed entering, maneuvering in, around and emerging from large bodies of water all over the world for hundreds of years. This chapter covers only a small cross-section of the most unusual incidents.

USOs vary in size and shape, but the most common are reported to be disc-shaped, cigar-shaped or cylindrical. They move at speeds far exceeding any Earth-based underwater craft, traveling anywhere between 150 and 500 knots (approx. 172 and 575 mph) when submerged, and some have been reported at speeds greater than that.

But what are they doing here? Do they have the same motives for their presence in our waters as UFOs that are active in the air? Are they departing from and returning to underwater bases where alien beings live and work? Are they using the water in an attempt to hide from curious bystanders and Earth's militaries? Are they sampling and studying Earth's natural resources? We don't know for sure, but in his book, *Undersea UFO Base: An In-Depth Investigation of USOs in the Santa Catalina Channel*,[47] UFO investigator Preston Dennett has presented some of the most well-documented incidents of unidentified craft in and around bodies of water.

Historic USO sightings

The 1492 Light Sighting was a possible USO seen during the first voyage of Christopher Columbus on October 11, 1492, by crew members shortly before the landing on Guanahani Island. The light was reported in Columbus' journal *Vita del Ammiraglio (The Life of the Admiral)* and by other sources. Columbus described the light as "a small wax candle that rose and lifted up, which to a few seemed to be an indication of land."

On June of 1845, according to the *Malta Times*, "We find the Brigantine Victoria some 900 miles east of Adalia when her crew saw three luminous bodies emerge from the sea into the air. They were visible for ten minutes flying a half mile from the ship." There were other witnesses who saw the same USO phenomenon from Adalia, Syria and Malta. The luminous bodies each displayed an apparent diameter larger than the size of the full moon.

Modern USOs

Commissioned on October 27, 1945, from the New York naval shipyard, the 1,000-foot long, 64,000-ton USS Franklin Delano Roosevelt was one of the first ships in the U.S. Navy's fleet to carry nuclear weapons. During its thirty-two years of service, it seemed to be a magnet for UFOs and USOs that were witnessed by many members of its crews on different occasions. One of the most interesting took place one evening in September 1958, near Guantanamo Bay, Cuba, at about 9:00 p.m. Several of the crew members spotted an unidentified, silent,

[47] Dennett, Preston. *Undersea UFO Base: An In-Depth Investigation of USOs in the Santa Catalina Channel.* Blue Giant Books. 2018.

fast-moving cigar-shaped craft rise from the water a distance away and approach parallel to the ship, close enough that they could feel heat coming off of it on their faces. They reported that they could see a row of windows on the side and non-human beings inside the craft looking back at them. The craft then turned bright orange in color and shot off into space. Of the approximately twenty-five members of the crew who witnessed the USO, most were quickly transferred off the FDR, and it was later discovered that the ship's logbook for that day had been altered to expunge the incident.

On February 10, 1951, Commander Graham Bethune, U.S. Navy, was flying his military plane from Iceland to Newfoundland when he saw a USO coming out of the water. He was about three hundred miles from his destination when he and his crew saw a glow on the water that looked like they were approaching a city at night.

> *"As we approached this glow it turned into a monstrous circle of white lights on the water. Then we saw a yellow halo, much smaller than whatever it was launched from, about 15 miles away. As the UFO approached my plane and flew alongside it, we could see the domed craft which had a corona discharge."*

In July 1967, a Dutch multi-national businessman, Adrian Beers, claimed that while sailing his yacht in the waters of the Oosterscheldt (the southwestern delta of the Netherlands), he collided with an alien craft in the water. He met the extraterrestrial pilots who told him they came from a planet called Iarga, ten light years from our Sun, and that they had been observing humans from the bottom of our oceans for many years. They then allowed him to visit their spacecraft in its underwater location and downloaded a massive amount of detailed information about their planet and their civilization to him. This event was documented in the book entitled, *UFO Contact from Planet Iarga: A Report of the Investigation*.[48]

Lake Casitas is located just inland of the coast in Ventura, at the northern end of the Santa Catalina Channel, California. One day in 1964, Frank Kinsey was at the lake on a fishing trip with his brother-in-law when they heard a loud sound of splashing water and witnessed an ob-

---

[48] Denaerde, Stefan & Stevens, Wendelle C. *UFO Contact from Planet Iarga: A Report of the Investigation.* Wendelle C. Stevens. 1982.

ject emerging from the water with such speed that it sucked up a large column of water that came loudly crashing down after it. Kinsey stated:

> "... It was a round object and it looked like it had a cone on top, where a person was looking out at us ... a being looking out at us ... I could see the eyes staring at us. I happened to have a pair of binoculars with me at the time. I picked them up and looked and could see a person looking out at me."

The object was about thirty feet wide, the outside perimeter appeared to be rotating, and the object was emitting a painfully loud noise. Kinsey noted several portholes around the top cone section of the object, and it was through one of these that he saw the being looking out at him. Kinsey further stated that the window:

> "... looked like it was real thick, heavy glass of some kind, or maybe it might have been a plastic of some kind. It has a gleam to it, it had a shine to it, like nothing I've ever seen. I've seen a lot of metals here on earth that had a high gloss, but nothing like this that I've ever seen." [49]

Suddenly, the object accelerated, glowing lavender and then bright orange-yellow, and in a few seconds it was fifteen miles away, and then it disappeared over the mountains.

Another incident took place in January 1980, involving a small private plane piloted by Noah Felice, who was flying with his cousin from Catalina Island to Las Vegas. They noticed a strange object in the water and as they passed over it, they saw a figure on top of the object. Felice stated that it wasn't really a person, but it "wasn't not a person," and he didn't know what to think, so he decided to make a turn and come back around to get a better view. Suddenly, a beam of light shot out of the object and struck the plane and took control of it. Felice reported:

> "It was alive. It was like a liquid light. That's when the sound started shutting off. You couldn't feel the vibration ... and we got hit with a second beam ... The

---

[49] Dennett, Preston. *Undersea UFO Base: An In-Depth Investigation of UFOs in the Santa Catalina Channel.* Blue Giant Books. 2018.

inside of the airplane was glowing and I knew we were moving because the light was becoming more intense. And it seemed as though we had passed through not a physical doorway, but a doorway of a sort, or some sort of framework of light."[50]

At that point, Felice blacked out and the plane crashed into the ocean. The next thing he remembered, he was being rescued by a patrol boat. He survived, but unfortunately, his cousin didn't.

Many sightings of unidentified flying craft in and around the world's oceans have been reported by crews of the Russian and U.S. navies over the years, although they have nearly always been met with denial and secrecy. Recent reports by UFO researchers suggest that there is an on-going U.S. Navy effort to destroy any evidence linking that organization to the UFO phenomenon. The reports by UFO researchers of sightings being edited out of ships' logs confirm a considerable naval sensitivity to the phenomenon. Researchers have also reported that naval archives in Secaucus, New Jersey appear to have been sabotaged - documents are missing and files have purposely been mixed chronologically in order to prevent attempts to do meaningful research at the facility.

USOs under the ice

Apparently, USOs are not limited by the geography of the Earth or the condition of the waters they move about in. On several occasions, craft have been seen flying in and out of bodies of water that were choked with heavy ice coverings, as if the ice presented no barrier to them. After such reports, large holes were observed in the ice, and it has been proposed that the craft may possess the ability to melt ice at the speed of transit. Examples of this have allegedly occurred in Norway, Sweden and Russia, where these objects have been reported entering and emerging from bodies of waters in the area.[51]

In an article entitled *"UFOs - at 450 Fathoms!"*[52] reporter Ed Hyde

---

[50] Ibid.

[51] *USOs - Unidentified Submerged Objects*, www.tarrdaniel.com/documents/Ufology/uso.html.

[52] Hyde, Ed. *U.F.O.s – at 450 Fathoms!* Man's Illustrated. March 1966.

told of a sighting made by Dr. R. J. Villela, a Brazilian scientist, who saw a UFO smash through an estimated forty feet of ice at the South Pole and soar into the sky at what he described as amazing speed.

USO nests

The Tully Saucer Nest case is sometimes known as Australia's Roswell because it has created so much controversy over the years. On January 19, 1966, George Peddly, a farmer living in Tully, Australia, was driving his tractor on his neighbor's property that was bordered by a lagoon about six feet deep, with tall reeds growing in it. The tractor engine began to cut out and when Mr. Peddly stopped to check on it, he heard a high-pitched hissing noise coming from the direction of the lagoon. When he looked in the direction of the sound, he saw a disc-shaped metallic object rise up from the lagoon to a height of about thirty to forty feet and then take off at high speed. He described the object as like two massive dinner plates stacked atop one another, about thirty feet wide and twelve feet high. When the object was gone, he went to the lagoon to see if he could find out what it was and he was amazed to see a circular depression in flattened reeds about thirty feet wide on the surface of the water. The indentation was not uniformly flat, but had sloping edges, as you would expect to see if a concave shape, like the bottom of a saucer, had impacted on it.

Word of the strange craft got out and it became a media sensation with local and international coverage, and the phenomenon was dubbed a "flying saucer nest." Samples of the water from the lagoon were sent to the physics department of the University of Bristol for radiation testing, and samples from the center of the nest tested positive for beta radiation. Unfortunately, the samples mysteriously disappeared, but at least a half dozen other flying saucer nests were identified in the area.

Undersea bases

If ETs are coming and going through Earth's waters, it's logical that they may be utilizing some type of bases where they can rest, recharge and do whatever they came here for, but since no bases have been found on the shores of lakes and oceans, they must be located in the water. There are reports of undersea alien bases off the coast of several different countries - South America, Puerto Rico, Russia, Scotland, the Patagonia Coast, Argentina, the Azores Islands, Portugal, Spain, the Canary Islands, Canada, Japan, the Dominican Republic, Norway, Newfoundland and the United States. Are those installations newly built or are they ancient structures, and are the beings who utilize them part of an underwater civilization or civilizations that evolved here? Or are they intelligent entities from other worlds who have been coming here for thousands of years and merely prefer to use the bottom of the ocean from which to operate?

In May 2014, Jimmy Church, of Dark Matter Radio, was contacted by a gentleman who claimed that while researching on Google Earth, he had noticed a large underwater structure three miles off the southern California coast. Church reported:

> "A massive underwater entrance has been discovered off the Malibu, California coast at Point Dume, which appears to be the Holy Grail of UFO/USO researchers, that have been looking for it over the last forty years. The plateau structure is 1.35 miles by 2.45 miles wide, 6.66 miles from land, and the entrance between the support pillars is 2,745 feet wide and 639 feet tall. It also has what looks like a total nuclear bomb proof ceiling that is 500 feet thick."

The fact that there is a huge structure of some kind in that location visible on Google Earth cannot be denied; but is it truly anomalous or is it natural? A member of the U.S. Geological Survey who examined the Google Earth pictures in 2014 and other geologists who have done so since, believe it is part of the continental shelf, representative of the naturally occurring geology in the area. But many Ufologists disagree and think it might be the entrance to an ancient alien base or tunnel system that may even be linked to an opening into the center of the Earth.

Numerous sightings of strange lights entering and exiting the sea around Puffin Island, Wales, has led some Ufologists to believe the area may be home to an underwater alien base. Experiencers from near the area have reported abductions by humanoids who told them they came from an undersea base near the island. There are even some theories that the area itself may be the ancient legendary kingdom of Cantre'r Gwaelod, an ancient sunken kingdom said to have occupied a tract of fertile land in Cardigan Bay to the west of Wales, which has been described as a Welsh Atlantis.

According to a former U.S. Marine who served at Guantanamo Bay in the late 1960s, there is an underwater alien base off the Cuban coast, the U.S. military is aware of it and has even managed to capture photographs of several alien craft entering and exiting the water there. He also states that he and his colleagues were under strict instructions not to talk about the strange activity they witnessed. The Marine claimed that the craft he saw appeared to be made of dull-colored metal with blue lights which would grow fainter and fainter after the craft entered the water, suggesting to him that whatever the object was, it was descending deeper into the water.

Lake Baikal in Siberia is said to be the deepest lake on the planet, with a history of UFO activity as well as alleged sightings of aliens underneath the water. Former Soviet naval officer and Ufologist Vladimir Azhazha claimed to have leaked top secret files relating to an incident in 1982 in which he stated that military divers on standard training exercises in the area witnessed a huge underwater craft in the lake moving with a speed they had never seen before. Several days later, they witnessed several strange beings under the water clad in shiny suits and what appeared to be small, advanced oxygen masks. According to the alleged leaked documents, the unit was ordered to capture these strange creatures, but when they attempted to do so, they were fought off with an advanced sonar wave weapon that killed three of the seven divers. The remaining four, terrified and injured, retreated. In 2009, photographs taken from the International Space Station seemed to show two distinct saucer-shaped anomalies in the region, fueling further speculation that an extraterrestrial presence was under Lake Baikal, and even the possibility that these "saucers" were the craft that had been witnessed nearly three decades earlier by the Soviet diving unit.

There is also a belief among some that USOs emerge from inside the Hollow Earth or have their origins in the super advanced ancient city of Atlantis which may lie somewhere in the depths of the Atlantic ocean. Many folks living along the Indian coastline have also witnessed bright colorful lights in the sky, particularly right before the 2004 tsunami hit the eastern coast.

To date, there is no definitive evidence to prove that there are underwater bases on Earth hosting extraterrestrial craft or beings;

however, in an article by blogger Agent K of *The Object Report*,[53] a very reputable government insider who worked in a classified capacity for Hughes Aircraft Corporation told him that "the military is directly involved with these aliens and they even have an underwater base in the San Pedro Basin near Catalina Island where they work with the Grays."

Effects of USOs

Dead fish are sometimes noticed after a USO is seen diving into or emerging from a body of water, causing speculation that propulsion systems that use high energy electrical systems may be the cause. On February 19, 1982, a USO plunged into Lake Lácar in Argentina and shortly thereafter, a large number of dead fish were observed floating in the lake. Samples of the fish were sent to a nearby government laboratory for autopsy and the fishes' air bladder systems were found to be compressed, supposedly by some type of shock wave. It was concluded that rapid movement of the USO may have been to blame.

When it comes to USOs, we don't really know any more about them than we know about UFOs, and the sad truth is that we know more about the surface of Mars than about our own oceans, which cover 70% of our planet. But obviously, it's not enough to just keep our eyes on the skies. We must keep our eyes on Earth's waters too.

"I contend that if we will only stick to being logical, there is no reason (a) why there could not be an extremely advanced 'civilization' under water, (b) why it might not be up to twice as old as ours, (c) why it should not have developed what we call space flight, and (d) why it should not be so far in advance of us technically."

Ivan T. Sanderson

---

[53] www.theobjectreport.com.

29

Q: Are experiencers and starseeds the same?

They can be, but they aren't always. In the UFO field, experiencers and starseeds both have contact with extraterrestrial beings, but in very different ways. And it can be confusing, especially for individuals who believe they may be one or the other.

Experiencers

As discussed in Chapter 1, an experiencer is an individual who has had contact with extraterrestrial or interdimensional beings. Such contact is widely varied and yet similar in many respects. Some experiences are traumatic and difficult, and some are positive and uplifting, but in most cases the ETs choose the time and place, and experiencers have no choice in either. It can be very challenging.

Experiencers cannot be defined by logistics – they are male and female, young and old, and come from different locations, cultures and societies around the world. Educational, religious and economic status appear to make no difference in whether an individual is of interest to alien beings.

Some experiencers are open to contact and even welcome it, while others would give nearly anything to make it stop and prevent it happening again. By and large, they are normal human beings who find themselves caught up in something which, in most cases, they can't explain and may not know how to deal with.

There have been human experiencers as long as alien beings have been on the Earth - probably before recorded time - and most of the knowledge humanity possesses about otherworldly beings has come from them. Without experiencers, there would be no UFO phenomenon.

Starseeds

Starseeds are quite different. The term generally describes a being from another planet who is born and lives as a human being on Earth with a specific mission or goal that guides and informs their life here. There are some variations, but two types seem to be most common.

One type of starseed is a highly advanced soul who incarnates into a fully human body for the purpose of assisting humanity and the Earth in the process of ascension to a higher level of spiritual development. The other type of starseed is a genetic mix of human and extraterrestrial in a human form - a human-alien hybrid - from a specific ET group or family, here for the purpose of completing some type of mission.

Throughout history, there have been unusually gifted human beings, intellectual geniuses or especially talented people who have brought knowledge to humanity in many areas. In ancient times, they were called wizards or saints, but many of them very likely were starseeds - advanced souls born into either fully human or human-alien hybrid bodies for the purpose of moving humanity along in some way.

While their origins may differ, both types of starseeds find their human experiences to be pretty much the same and have much in common. They are born of human mothers into typical families and cultures, and although unusual things tend to happen to them, most starseeds lead seemingly normal human lives.

Starseeds are typically very intuitive, curious, open to developing psychic and spiritual abilities and fascinated with spirituality, the higher realms and cosmic knowledge. They tend to be shy and introverted as children, and often prefer their own company to the company of their peers or adults. They often feel out-of-place in daily situations, like they don't belong in their families and social circles, or like they are different from everyone around them, without understanding why. There may be some anatomical and physiological differences between a starseed and his or her earthly family, but for the most part, they have normal human bodies.

Starseeds may have no recollection of their true origin when they are young and may go well into adulthood that way. However, it is said that the genes of starseeds are encoded with "wake-up call" designed to activate recall of their origins at a predetermined moment in life. Many starseeds will experience synchronicities, such as 11:11,[54] as their wake-up call. The starseed awakening process can be gentle and happen gradually as one walks a spiritual path of self-exploration, or it can be very dramatic and abrupt, sometimes occurring during a

---

[54] https://www.dimension1111.com.

major transitional phase of their life. After that, recollections of their origin and mission begin to become clear and connection to their higher selves is also strengthened, which allows them to further understand who they are and why they are here. As this knowledge begins to unfold, it can be confusing and unsettling, and some starseeds find counseling or therapy to be helpful in bringing forward and clarifying whatever knowledge and memories are coming through.

Starseeds often feel a sense of urgency or have a feeling that something important is about to happen. Although they can't explain what it is, they may get a nagging feeling that they are supposed to remember something - like they are "remembering the future."

While the eventual goal for the starseed is to become fully aware of their purpose and mission on Earth and be able to do the work they agreed to do, their soul memory usually returns by varying degrees, depending on their level of conscious awareness and their particular path and mission. The time it takes for their memory to return allows their personal connection to their higher self and ability to be guided by their intuition and inner knowing to strengthen.

Because many starseeds have had similar missions on other planets and are familiar with the procedures and techniques necessary for raising their personal vibration and consciousness, they may already be capable of ridding themselves of limiting behavioral patterns and fears that might take non-starseeds many lifetimes to accomplish. This is of great benefit to their present lifetime.

All starseeds come to Earth with a mission, and there are many different kinds of missions, but all starseeds know what they are getting into before they agree to be born on Earth, and they take on the human experience willingly. Some missions are strictly spiritual, such as using their psychic or advanced spiritual abilities to assist other enlightened Earth souls to anchor light to Mother Earth, or to release the souls of human beings who have died and are trapped on Earth. Some starseeds act more in the physical realm, observing life around them and reporting back to their ET group or family what they experience in their daily lives, or assisting humanity on a practical level as teachers, artists, enlightened scientists or medical professionals.

The Appendix section of this book contains some of the most commonly reported characteristics of starseeds. Of course, they are merely guidelines and do not guarantee that someone is a starseed.

Millions of people are experiencers who have had contact with beings from other worlds. Some may be starseeds and human-alien hybrids who actually come from the stars, and some may be fully human beings whose origins are on Earth and who have contact with alien beings here. Technically, there are differences among them, but what links them all to each other are their humanity and consciousness.

"Some part of our being knows this is where we came from. We long to return. And we can. Because the cosmos is also within us. We're made of star-stuff. We are a way for the cosmos to know itself."

Carl Sagan

Q: Are alien abductions actually OBEs
or something else ?

"I stood at the foot of the king-size bed viewing myself and John asleep. To my left stood a three to four-foot form (human like) standing next to the sleeping John. The form appeared expressionless and stationary, attired in a grey body suit without any reaction from me. I floated (about ten feet) to the bedroom window. My light weight hand lifted the shade slat to view the backyard. Below the window there was a fifty-foot circular craft hovering a few feet from the treeless ground. There were multi-colored lights underneath the craft. I could see a circular beamed light on the ground with an opening at the bottom of the craft. About a dozen people were walking and floating towards the beamed light dressed in bedtime clothes. I recall feeling amazed that I didn't know my neighbors were involved with unidentified flying objects. Within a flash I lifted instantly with a swish through the roof to join the others entering the craft." JS

This is a valid question, although experiencers of both phenomena may be loath to consider the possibility. Researchers who closely examine typical out-of-body experiences (OBEs) and alien abductions find astounding similarities between them, but OBEs explained as psychological or neurological conditions are generally more acceptable than alien abductions. At the same time, based on physical evidence and experiencer testimonials, it's not reasonable to believe that all alien abductions are OBEs or that all OBEs are alien abductions.

Alien abductions

As discussed elsewhere in this book, an alien abduction is an event in which a person is taken against his or her will by alien beings and then returned to the original location sometime later. This type of event may involve being subjected to experiments and tests, reproductive procedures, educational activities and being given messages to relay back to specific individuals or to humanity as a whole. Abductions can take place at any time, but are most commonly reported at night. The human subject may be conscious or unconscious during the experience and may have full memory, partial memory or no memory of it later. While no two abduction events are exactly the same, typical scenarios are reported and the aftermaths may be negative or positive. Contrary to popular belief, abductions are not the only types of human-ET contact reported; indeed, they are not even the most common.

It's important to acknowledge that some researchers and experiencers believe all alien abductions are hoaxes perpetrated by humans, and that genuine alien beings do not abduct humans. Whether they are right or not, the truth is that countless human beings have had, and continue to have, experiences that they describe as alien abductions, which makes them undeniably part of the human-ET contact phenomenon.

OBEs

An OBE is usually defined as an experience in which a person seems to perceive the world from a location outside their physical body. It has been estimated that one in ten people have had an OBE once, or more commonly, several times in their life. When the FREE Study asked the question, *"Have you had an Out of Body Experience?"*, out of 1,524 participants, 1,201 said *Yes*, while only 323 said *No*.

The term "out-of-body experience" was introduced by parapsychologist, G. N. M. Tyrrell, in his book, *Apparitions*,[55] in 1943. In 1958, Robert Monroe had the experience of floating out of his body for the first time and later, in 1971, he wrote his seminal work, *Journeys out of the Body*,[56] which launched the phrase "out-of-body experience" into the public conversation. Although this was the first popular discussion of OBEs, the phenomenon had been described since ancient times by many others using the terms "astral projection," "soul travel" and "spirit walking."

Studies published in 1886 describing alleged cases of OBEs ad-

---

[55] Tyrrell, G.N.M. *Apparitions.* Gerald Duckworth and Co. Ltd. 1943.

[56] Monroe, Robert A. *Journeys Out of the Body.* Doubleday, 1971. Reprint Broadway Books. 2001.

vocated an "etheric body" concept. The etheric body is considered the first, or lowest, layer of the human energy field or aura, whose purpose is to sustain and connect the physical body with its higher bodies. Other researchers and occult writers supported a view describing the phenomenon of the OBE experience in terms of bilocation, in which an etheric body can release itself from the physical body and, essentially, exist in two places at the same time. James Baker[57] wrote that during an OBE, a mental body enters an "intercosmic region." Some researchers believe that OBEs are the projection of the spiritual body from the physical body for the purpose of the soul's purification.

Out-of-body experiences were known, during the Victorian period in spiritualist literature, as "travelling clairvoyance" and "psychical excursions." In the 19th century, OBEs became a popular topic of the romantic literary movement and, not surprisingly, were eagerly discussed by early psychical researchers.

> "I suddenly seemed to divide into two distinct beings. [...] One of these beings remained motionless on the sofa; the other could move some little distance, and could actually look at the motionless body on the sofa."
> Journal of Society for Psychical Research, July 1894.

In addition to paranormal and spiritual explanations, there may be a variety of physiological and psychological theories for out-of-body experiences, including brain traumas, dehydration, sensory deprivation, use of psychedelic drugs, electrical stimulation of the brain, and sleep, among others. Mainstream neuroscientists and psychologists regard OBEs as dissociative experiences arising from psychological and neurological factors. Such states can also be deliberately induced using certain technology and meditative and thought control techniques.

Individuals experiencing OBEs sometimes report that they are preceded or initiated by a lucid dream state. In many cases, people who claim to have had an OBE report being on the verge of sleep or already asleep shortly before the experience; often in situations where the sleep was not particularly deep, possibly due to illness, environmen-

---

[57] Baker, James, Jr. The exteriorization of the mental body: a scientific interpretation of the out-of-the-body experience known as pneumakinesis. William-Frederick Press. 1954.

tal noises, emotional stress, exhaustion from overworking, frequent re-awakening, etc. About half of them note that a feeling of sleep paralysis was involved.

Near-death experiences

Another form of spontaneous OBE is the near-death experience (NDE) which some individuals report having had at times of severe physical trauma such as near-drownings, automobile accidents or during major surgery.

An NDE typically begins as an OBE, but then goes on to include visions of deceased relatives, an experience of transcending ego and space-time boundaries, a feeling of peace and painlessness, having the sense of moving up or through a narrow passageway or a long tunnel toward a bright, white light, encountering "beings of light" and a God-like figure or similar entities, being given a "life review" and often a choice of whether or not to return to their current physical life. An individual may also be instructed that he or she needs to make changes when they return to their life or given messages to relay to people in their life when they return. Some individuals have reported returning from the experience with new knowledge or increased psychic and/or healing abilities.

Similarities between OBEs and abductions

Probably the best source of comparative information on alien abductions and OBEs is found in the study, *With the Eyes of the Mind: An Empirical Analysis of Out-of-Body States,*[58] by Gabbard and Twemlow (the "GT Study"), which sets out some of the most common features of alien abduction and OBEs. Among other things, the GT Study found that:

• 94% of people who had OBEs say the experience was "more real than a dream" and had a "physical" quality to it. Likewise, alien abductions are also viewed as physical occurrences. The abductee may report being in an altered state of consciousness during the event, but the overall experience is described as physical.

• 76% of OBE subjects report that their body image during an

---

[58] Gabbard, Glen O. & Twemlow, Stuart W. *With the Eyes of the Mind: An Empirical Analysis of Out-of-Body States.* Praeger Publishers. 1984.

Q: Are alien abductions actually OBEs or something else?

OBE was identical to or very similar to their normal physical body. During alien abductions, experiencers often report physical examinations or experiments being done on their normal physical body.

• 37% of individuals said they were aware of the presence of other beings during their OBEs, often describing them as "non-physical" beings. During alien abductions, experiencers typically see and interact with alien beings, but some also describe seeing "non-physical" beings.

• 26% of people felt the presence of "spirit guides," "helpers" or "friends" during OBEs. Some abductees or contactees also describe the ETs as guides or helpers. "The alien beings function as spirit energies or guides, serving the evolution of consciousness and identity."

• During OBEs, it's very common for a person to seemingly pass through physical matter, such as reaching for a doorknob and having their hand go through it, or walking through a wall or floating up through a ceiling. In abduction experiences, it's very common for subjects to describe being lifted into the air and passing through walls and ceilings.

• OBE subjects often say their sense of time becomes distorted during their experience, as if time had stopped for them, much like the missing time often reported in alien abduction and contact experiences. One abductee described how he "experienced the collapse of past, present, and future."

Other similarities between OBEs and alien abductions have been reported.

• At the onset of an OBE, a subject often feels they are paralyzed. This has been explained by therapists as sleep paralysis, a commonly reported feature of alien abductions.

• People having OBEs typically are able to float and defy the laws of gravity, and may describe flying or gliding as well. Abductees commonly float up out of their beds and into alien craft or to other locations.

• During OBEs, individuals sometimes report communicating telepathically with other humans or spirit beings. During alien abductions, experiencers almost always report any communication that takes place with ETs as telepathic.

• Many people who have OBEs feel as if they are leading a double life or have one foot in everyday reality and the other foot in an alternate reality. Many experiencers also talk about leading a double life or living in two different dimensions or two different realities.

Differences between OBEs and abductions

Despite the similarities between OBEs and alien abduction experiences, there are obvious and very important differences between the two.

• An OBE requires only one human being, whereas an abduction requires at least one human being and one or more alien beings.

• Control - OBE experiencers typically have more control of their situation than alien abductees. During an OBE, an individual can often go where they want to go in the environment without feeling that they are under the control of another power. If they want to move around in the environment or even relocate to another place, they often can. In abductions, the individual usually feels powerless to help himself and may, in fact, be paralyzed and unable to move.

• Physical Evidence - OBEs don't usually generate physical evidence, but abductees/contactees often report physical evidence left on their bodies after experiences in the form of bruises, burns, scoop marks or scars, and marks on the ground, trees or plants, automobiles, etc., where landings or events took place.

• Eyewitnesses - OBEs, in which a person's spirit or astral body temporarily leaves their physical body, are subjective experiences. Since the spirit isn't usually visible, even if there is another person with them, the experience will not be witnessed. Alien abductions, on the other hand, are physical experiences that may be witnessed by others who are not abducted.

• Pain - OBEs are typically painless events, at times blissful, and are even sometimes used as a release from painful situations; however, they are seldom, if ever, described as painful or traumatic. During OBEs, subjects may observe their bodies being operated on by human doctors, but because they are separated from their physical bodies, they don't feel pain. In addition, people who experience OBEs don't typically report medical-type procedures or experiments being performed on them, unless the procedure is the cause of the OBE. Unfortunately, during alien abductions, many individuals report being subjected to painful physical procedures.

Alien abductions and OBEs?

After decades of investigation and research, and testimonies of thousands of individuals involved in the human-ET contact phenomenon, it's clear that alien abduction experiences are real. Likewise, years of research and reports back up countless descriptions of OBEs. In most cases, these two human experiences are distinctly different, but sometimes they cross over, with ET contact experiences containing characteristics of both. The opening quote of this chapter describes such an experience. The one thing they do have in common, however, is consciousness – human consciousness and alien consciousness. Human beings are conscious beings and, from what we know of the ETs who have interacted with us on Earth since before recorded time, some ETs are conscious beings too.

ETs and the paranormal - separate or overlapping realms?

Traditionally, UFO investigators have kept the fields of "extraterrestrial" and "paranormal" events separate. But increasing reports of individuals who are encountering both extraterrestrial beings and the spirits of dead human beings in the same events are bringing that practice into question, along with the boundaries of reality, space and time.

In addition to others, the author Whitley Strieber believes there is a link of some kind between the realm of extraterrestrial beings and the world of the dead. In an interview, he shared the following story of a reader who contacted him with an amazing experience:

> *"He and his wife are in the living room, the old dog is asleep on the hearth, it's late at night, 10 o'clock or so at night. Suddenly the dog becomes very agitated and the dog needs to go out again, for the second time, which is very unusual for this dog. The wife goes to take the dog out and opens the door and as she does, she sees a fireball race across the sky and go down behind the trees in front of the house and she says to her husband 'I just saw a plane going down in flames and you're going to get*

a call,' because he's with the FAA. Just at that time, their little seven-year-old boy comes running down the stairs shouting 'Mommy, Daddy, Mommy, Daddy! Little blue men came into my room and they had Bobby with them and he said to tell you that he's all right.' Bobby was the older son who had died in an auto accident a week before."

Was this merely a young boy's emotional response to the recent death of his brother and a fireball in the sky? Or was it truly a visit from little blue extraterrestrial men and the spirit of his recently-deceased brother?

In the same interview, Strieber also talks about how during his first encounter with alien beings, he was surprised to see that, in addition to the ETs in attendance, there was a man there who he knew, but hadn't seen in over a year. He was even more surprised, however, when he later learned that the man had died nearly ten months before he was seen in the contact experience. Was it really the spirit of the man who Strieber had known? Or was there something in the contact experience that connected Whitley with the man through their consciousness?

The famous Scole Experiments were a series of séances that took place in England from 1993 to 1998. The experiments were conducted in the village of Scole, in the region of Norfolk, in the basement of a farmhouse that came to be called the "Scole Hole." The experiments received so much attention that the prestigious Society for Psychical Research asked to observe, test, record and film what took place. For most of the experiments, the camera was placed on a tripod in the darkened room, positioned before two mirrors. At the end of each session, the team would examine the film footage, and they often saw that the camera had repeatedly and impossibly zoomed in and out on its own. They noted that the tapes contained weird scenes, smiling faces, vibrant colors and hints of body parts moving across the screen in a red light. However, the most unusual tape showed a pink and gold line running horizontally across the screen which pivoted to reveal a square set on its edge. As it rotated, it was seen to contain an image. According to the Scole team "This was a very clear view of an animated interdimensional friend, whose features, to say the least, were not exactly as our own." They called their new friend "Blue" and the image was identical to the image of the classic Gray alien. Another example of an overlap between the realms of ETs and the paranormal?

Q: Are alien abductions actually OBEs or something else?

Alien abductions appear to demonstrate that ETs possess the ability to navigate and possibly manipulate space, time and different dimensions and planes of existence, and perhaps even what we have traditionally thought of as the spirit world. OBEs and NDEs may demonstrate human beings' ability to do likewise. Perhaps they all indicate that we are really doing the same thing, just not in exactly the same way.

> "It's more likely that alien abductions and OBEs are merely two different approaches to the same thing: exploration of our multi-dimensional universe that both humans and alien beings inhabit."
>
> Robert Peterson

31

Q: Love and sex . . . with aliens?

"Now is the time. The time when my lover comes. I long for him. I am only half without him. I close my eyes and recall the last time we were together. His body, his spirit, the knowing we share as with no one else. As I lie down to sleep, I can feel him approaching. There is a sensation in the air around me. He is finally here and nothing else matters. In the blink of an eye, a single beat of my heart, we are on the ship. The ship moves and I am joined with it. The Others move and I am joined with them. My lover moves and we are one again. The breathless exhilaration of union. Timeless, mindless, we move through endless space. I am human and yet my human experience can never express the overpowering, overwhelming passion and purity of this. I know that only fragments of memories will be left when it is over, but the essence of love, deep peace and endless knowing will remain until he comes again." PL

This beautiful poem was written by a life-long experiencer who has a romantic relationship with an alien being. She is a sane, healthy woman who was first abducted by ETs when she was a child. There were no more contacts until she was an adult, when the visits resumed, intensified, and a special relationship with one of the alien beings developed into love. The passion and longing she feels for her lover and the joy she finds in his company are obvious from the way she writes about him, and can be understood by anyone who has ever been in love. She usually keeps her feelings private, but made an exception here. She adds:

"As you can imagine, being in love with someone from another world can be tough for a lot of reasons, but it's part of my life. I never want to lose him or the extraordinary experiences he brings me. My life is beyond remarkable."

The book, *Beyond The Light Barrier: The Autobiography of Elizabeth Klarer,* [59] tells the story of a South African woman who was taken aboard a spaceship by a being named Akon, from a planet in the Proxima Centauri system. Elizabeth states that from the first moment she saw him on the ship, she felt a deep bond with him and knew they were meant to be together.

> *"A deep emotion and great happiness spread its warmth through my mind and body. The wondrous reality was almost too much for me, and I could not find words adequate to express the fullness of love within my heart for this man from another planet."*

Their relationship was deep and passionate on both physical and spiritual levels as Elizabeth traveled with Akon to his home planet, Meton. She bore him a son and lived as a member of his family there until she was returned to Earth, where she eventually lived out her life happily, with her human family and with frequent visits from Akon and their son.

On several occasions, human experiencers have described intensely erotic, but also deeply emotional, experiences of lovemaking with alien beings. Comparing the experience to sex with a human, one individual said:

> *"I felt sex, but there was this intense feeling all through me, and then peacefulness, and then I felt loved. It was different than sex with a human being. Physical sex. It wasn't just on the outside. It was more internal. I know this is going to sound dumb - but it's like having spiritual sex. . . . There's a lot of ego involved in sex with a human being. You're thinking a lot of thoughts while you're having sex, such as if this doesn't finish off good, we're both gonna feel funny later or whatever. . . . It's too technical. So with these beings there's none of this 'okay we have to have a certain amount of foreplay, we have to do this and that'. It was just like a connection, a spiritual connection. "*

---

[59] Klarer, David. *Beyond The Light Barrier: The Autobiography of Elizabeth Klarer.* Light Technology Publishing. 2009.

John Mack relates one abductee's days and months of contact in which he participated in repeated episodes of lovemaking with the same alien female, but he didn't feel raped and abused. Instead, he felt very closely bonded to her and said of her, "It feels like she's my real wife - I want to say on a soul level."

Human love

Most human beings fall in love at least once in their lifetime and, happily or unhappily, it's one of the deepest emotional experiences of their lives. Indeed, the emotion of love is so important to our species that much of our great literature, favorite films, most enduring works of art and nearly every pop song ever written express our preoccupation with it. And yet, the power that this state of mind holds over us, especially when it occurs for the first time, is still one of life's great mysteries.

Beyond the basic drive to perpetuate the species, scientists in fields ranging from anthropology to neuroscience have differing theories as to why human beings fall in love and why we fall in love with the people we fall in love with. Indeed, many people say they don't really know why they fell in love with someone; there was "just something about her" or "something special that drew us together." Indeed, many of us spend a lifetime searching for that "special something." Do those same theories hold true in the case of human beings who fall in love with aliens?

Love is sometimes called a drug - and for good reason. When we fall in love, our brains release a powerful cocktail of chemicals, including, among others, dopamine and norepinephrine, which create feelings of euphoria and pleasure, making us want to remain close to the object of our affection. The neurotransmitter, serotonin, normally provides us with a sense of being in control, but when we fall in love, its level in the brain drops, which causes our sense of control to decrease. When that happens, the term "crazy in love" may not be too far from the truth, as we can become obsessively fixated on the other person and lose our ability to focus on anything but them. At the same time, the prefrontal cortex, our brain's reasoning, command and control center, shifts into low gear, and the amygdala (a key component of the brain's threat response system) also shifts down. When we are engaged in romantic love, the neural machinery responsible for making critical assessments of those with whom we are romantically involved is less efficient, which essentially is the neural basis for the ancient wisdom "love is blind."

That's how humans function in love, but what about ETs? Many experiencers claim that alien beings lack emotions, which may be the reason they are interested in humanity. At the same time, other experiencers report that certain ET types, those often reported interacting with human children, do have emotions. But is it really love or something else?

Alien-human love or alien control?

After the thousands of years that ETs have been studying and interacting with humanity on Earth, they likely have a thorough understanding of the function of our brains and may be capable of manipulating and controlling us to achieve their objectives. Many experiencers have reported this as possible. If so, is it also possible for an alien being to control the chemistry of a human brain to make that individual fall in love, thereby diminishing instinctive fear, altering judgment and making them more compliant?

Most of us would agree that there is probably nothing riskier than falling in love, and yet we do it anyway. How much more risk is involved in giving one's heart to an alien being? Can real, true love exist between humans and aliens or are they merely using our emotions for their own purposes?

Alien-human sex

Otherworldly beings seem very interested in human sex. Many individuals report having sexual experiences during alien abduction events that involve the removal of sperm and ova, ostensibly for study, testing or use in experimentation or human-alien hybridization programs. And some individuals recall being taken aboard alien craft where they participated in sexual intercourse with aliens or other humans, willingly or unwillingly. It's not surprising that unwilling participants often describe their experiences as abhorrent and terrifying, while others declare them "the best sex I ever had!" What accounts for the difference? Even though it may be difficult to accept, the answer likely involves the human's belief system and prior life experiences as well as the ET's behavior.

While many sexual experiences are reported taking place aboard alien ships, some humans who claim to have sexual relations with otherworldly beings say they are never taken aboard ships, and describe their relationships as very different from typical abduction-type experiences.

Simon Parkes claims that he has had a relationship with one particular alien being since he was six years old, who he describes as "a green creature, about 210 centimeters (7 ft.) tall, wearing a purple robe." He refers to her as the "Cat Queen" because she has a cat-like face, large eyes, small nostrils and a thin mouth. He claims that as he got older, the relationship became sexual and has produced at least one child - a daughter - and he continues to have sex with his ET mistress about four times a year. Although he is married, he doesn't see it as cheating on his human wife, because the relationship is not on a human level. It's his belief that "The reason why extraterrestrials are interested in me is not because of my physical body but what's inside - my soul."[60]

Painter David Huggins tells of experiencing contact with different types of beings from childhood, including short gray beings and a small Sasquatch-type being with glowing yellow eyes, but his first sexual encounter with a human-alien hybrid named Crescent was at age 17. He was walking in the country near his Georgia home when he encountered the alien being, who he describes as female with dark hair, large eyes and a pale, gray-colored, pointed face. She undressed, so Huggins did as well, and they had sex, quickly and quietly, with no feelings or emotions involved. He had no idea why he was chosen, but over the years, Crescent has returned to him again and again, with many of their sexual meetings observed by insect-like aliens that he identifies as "the leaders." He thinks of Crescent as his girlfriend and believes that he has fathered over fifty hybrid children with her over the years. He has also continued to see Grays, the small Sasquatch-type being with luminous, yellow eyes and insectoid beings during his meetings with Crescent. He has created hundreds of works of art depicting his experiences with Crescent and other beings, which he credits for helping him deal with the trauma of those experiences. He is also the subject of a documentary film entitled, *Love and Saucers:*

---

[60] *10 People Who Claim To Have Sexual Encounters With Aliens.* https://listverse.com.

The Far Out World of David Huggins,[61] in which he tells the story of his life, presents his art and tries to explain what his connection with extraterrestrials and the universe means to him and humanity.

Singer Pamela Stonebrooke claims to have had a number of erotic encounters with a reptilian alien. During her first encounter, she woke up one night aboard an alien ship with a being who initially appeared to be a handsome, well-built, blonde human male. It wasn't until mid-coitus that something changed: "All of a sudden, the energy felt totally different. It felt aggressive, and the entity felt bigger - bigger than the person who was inside me." But even though she realized that she was no longer having sex with a human male, by that time Pamela was beyond caring. "The telepathic communication was so intense and sensual and emotional. It was everything you would want to feel to be able to surrender in a sexual experience. It was almost like every cell in your body was having an orgasm."[62] After some other abduction experiences, she came to believe that she was being used as part of a human-alien hybridization program.

One of the most well-known human-alien sexual contact events took place in 1957 involving Antonio Villas-Boas, a Brazilian farmer, who was abducted onto a spaceship by four small alien beings on his farm one night. They undressed him, washed his body, took a sample of his blood and left him alone in a cell. After a short while, he was joined by a curious-looking female with almond-shaped eyes, high cheekbones, and a pointed chin, who had sex with him willingly, but who refused to kiss him, preferring instead to bite his chin and make animal noises. When the sexual act was done, she briefly pointed at her belly and then toward the sky and left the room. He followed her into another room, where the other beings were talking, but when he tried to steal a clock-like device as proof of his encounter, the beings ejected him from the ship. Although he had enjoyed the sex at the time, Antonio later stated: "All they wanted was a good stallion to improve their stock."[63]

[61] Abrahams, Brad, Ralston, Matt & Ibrahim, Grant. *Love and Saucers: The Far Out World of David Huggins.* Curator Pictures & Perceive Think Act Films. 2017.

[62] *10 People Who Claim To Have Sexual Encounters With Aliens.* https://listverse.com.

[63] Ibid.

How good is it?

Some humans find sex with alien beings very enjoyable and satisfying; those who are in love with their alien sexual partners certainly do. But most individuals who report sexual encounters with alien beings claim otherwise. In the first place, it's not logical to expect beings who have evolved on other planets or dimensions to be anatomically or physiologically compatible with Earth humans. Additionally, alien paramours are usually reported to be less interested in actual lovemaking and more interested in getting down to business with the sex act in order to extract sperm or do whatever else is crucial to completing their mission.

Interestingly, some experiencers have reported that when sexual activity was first initiated by aliens, they were lulled into a false sense of security by a flood of imagery in their minds in which "the abductee is made to believe that either her husband or loved one is with her. Abductees sometimes say that the face of the husband, for instance, tends to 'phase' in and out of the face of the alien."[64]

Not all individuals who have reported sexual experiences with aliens were given reasons why, but some were told that their DNA was being taken to be used in hybridization programs and, indeed, many individuals have reported being part of such studies and even later being taken for interaction with beings they were told were their hybrid offspring. Others believe aliens have a general interest in human anatomy and physiology, behavior and emotional states, and choose to study human sexuality because it's such an integral part of our basic human nature.

Another explanation

Stockholm Syndrome, also known as "capture bonding," refers to a group of psychological symptoms that occur in some persons who are abducted and held in captive or hostage situations, in which those individuals may express empathy, sympathy and positive feelings toward their captors, sometimes to the point of defending them, identifying with them and even feeling affection for them. It's a condition that can cause individuals to develop a psychological alliance with

---

[64] Jacobs, David. *Secret Life: Firsthand, Documented Accounts of UFO Abductions.* Fireside. 1993.

their captors as a survival strategy. The data for understanding Stockholm Syndrome have been derived from actual hostage situations that have occurred since 1973, which differ considerably from one another in location, number of people involved and time frame. Is it possible that some cases of human-alien love relationships could be forms of Stockholm Syndrome? It's natural for human beings to form bonds of trust with other humans in times of danger, uncertainty or stress, and as much as we might not like to think about it, there is no reason not to believe that in the right circumstances, it might be the same with alien beings who have the ability to control us or elicit our trust.

I am convinced that there are no more complex creatures in the universe than human beings, which is why otherworldly beings are so fascinated with us and why they aren't satisfied to merely observe from a distance, but have been interacting intimately with us for so long. In the process, they have made indelible impressions on humanity, touching us on our most intimate and primal levels. Is it really possible for human beings to fall in love with aliens or aliens to fall in love with humans? Why not?

"Do you think the universe fights for souls to be together? Some things are too strange and strong to be coincidences."

Emery Allen

32

Q: What do ETs think and feel about us?

Of all the questions I have been asked throughout the years about ETs and their motives for interacting with human beings on Earth, I am convinced that if we could find out what they truly think and feel about us, most of our other questions would be answered and we would have a much better understanding of this profound phenomenon as a whole. Whether the ETs in contact with humanity are free-will individuals guided by independent intelligence, thoughts and feelings, or automatons operating via blind programming, will determine how they approach us and what our contact with them will be like.

Throughout the long history of human-ET contact, for the most part, our alien visitors have remained silent with respect to what they think and feel about us. Why? Maybe they don't have the ability to communicate their thoughts and feelings. Maybe they follow protocols that don't permit communication. Maybe they consider us too intellectually inferior to understand them. Or maybe they simply don't think, feel or have opinions about us one way or the other.

Experiencers sometimes report that ETs do share their thoughts and feelings during contact events. Many of these messages are positive, assuring contactees that they respect and care for humanity and are here to offer guidance and support as we move toward an advanced future. Reports of channeled communications between ETs and non-experiencer humans have increased and much of the information received consists of positive messages of respect and support.

At the same time, others say the messages they are getting from alien beings present a darker picture of ET attitudes, motivations and intentions regarding humanity. Instead of positive messages, their communications betray motives and agendas that are anything but beneficial, and indicate that the aliens either have little regard for humanity or are actually out to destroy us.

Like many people, I have my own opinions about what our extraterrestrial visitors think and feel about us, but I don't profess to know for sure, so I reached out to a few people who have been involved in

the UFO/ET field for many years and asked them. They are researchers, therapists, investigators and experiencers. All of them are honest,
smart, common-sense and compassionate individuals. While they may
not agree with each other, if anyone has the inside track on what ETs
may be thinking and feeling about the human race, it's probably them.
Here are some of their thoughts.

*"What do ET's think of us, the people of Earth? I
think the answer depends to a great extent on whether
they are oriented to service to others or service to self.
As a generality, those oriented to service to others see us
as younger brothers and sisters on the spiritual journey
and stand ready to assist us on that journey when
circumstances permit them to do so without interfering in
our free will. On the other hand, those oriented to service
to self, seek to exploit us for their benefit without regard
for our free will or concern about the consequences to
us as a result of their exploitation of us. While these are
clearly defined polar opposite positions, it may well be
that some, if not many, ET groups are a mixture of both, in
varying degrees of dynamic tension. Any interaction with
ET groups calls for discernment and caution on the part of
Earth humanity; naiveté is not an option in dealing with
them." MN*

*"I think it depends on the race of beings. Most, I
feel, are seeing us on our revolutionary path as brave,
young adventurers who are surprising many members of
the universe with our ability to overcome hardship and
thousands of years of tyrannical slavery. Some feel we are
a waste of time and yet others feel we make a great entrée
with a nice glass of Chianti. Humans reflect the universe
and the universe reflects back." ME*

*"Certainly, there must be a good deal of variety
among ETs, and their agendas and attitudes toward us,
just as there is among we humans here on Earth toward
each other. In general, though, what ETs think and feel
about human beings may well be influenced by our own
thoughts, feelings, and beliefs - expressing what we*

expect, fear, or desire. For example, depending on the views of humans involved, some ETs may seem kindly or coldly matter-of-fact as they perform physical procedures upon those humans. Some ETs have also been reported as afraid of humans exploiting them physically. There have also been reports of ETs expressing surprise at the distress of some experiencers who have supposedly "forgotten" their agreement to participate in the contact." DJ

"I've been a life-long experiencer. I believe that all life is connected throughout the universe and that entities from other worlds much older and advanced than ours, care for planet Earth and always have since its creation. That being said, Earth has gone through a lot of changes since its beginning and so have all the creatures, including humans. I believe today's humans are the result of the manipulation of the evolutionary processes by ET entities and that we are the result of time, trial and experimentation by them that never ends. They take what they need to advance life in the universe. It is done without permission or awareness in most cases. I believe that the ETs would like to raise the human consciousness level and awareness so that we can join the universal Galactic Community and also save the planet from its unhealthy state to one of wellness, as it was meant to be. If we fail to do this as a human race, the planet will be chosen to survive over human life. We are replaceable to them. The ETs are very interested in us and study every aspect of the Earth human. Besides the nuts and bolts of human DNA and the interplanetary breeding project, they are particularly interested in sociology and our human nature. This is an important part of their understanding and decision making regarding us and our planet. We are they, they are we. We are one." KR

"The ET influence is a bag of mixed agendas. Some ETs have an honest and healthy respect for the human sovereignty of this planet, they are here to observe and study just as one intelligent species would study another. Limiting their contact and guarding their overall

193

influence. Humanity must evolve socially and morally at their own speed. Those are the good guys! Unfortunately, that's not the case with some. The reptilians and grays have a very different agenda, it doesn't include for the "good" of the current human race. The hybrid program is an excellent example of this. With an agenda of eventually dominating our world, it's not necessarily a bad thing I suppose (this is my opinion.) I'm not especially proud of human behavior as the dominant race currently in charge. The Reptilian agenda is the most mysterious and could fall either to the dark side or to the lighter side. I'm not sure. I'm sure there are others, perhaps trans-dimensional who are both benevolent and very spiritual or equally as "evil" and demonic. The mystery continues and only time will tell what they think and feel about us, but the human race must wake up to this reality. Our continued existence depends on it." JM

"I speak of my own experiences. I truly believe the other races that have "visited" planet Earth and have conducted abductions see us humans as inferior or mentally/spiritually fragile. My children and I have not been harmed. We are whole in the true sense of the word so then why the partial amnesia? I think the aliens in general think of us and treat us as if we were children that are not obeying their parents. Some aliens use us humans, others do not know what to think of us or what to do with us." SRC

"I think the ETs might feel about human beings as if we were an unresolved project whose creator left us unfinished, and that we are worth studying because of the way we have rallied back, and that we just might have potential enough to be a startlingly adaptive species that just might be worth saving. We can only hope for that." SW

We all would like to know the answer to the question, "What do ETs think and feel about us?" But if you're like me, you're too busy just trying to keep up with your daily life to worry about it. Perhaps one day the ETs will see fit to tell us themselves.

Q: What do ETs think and feel about us?

Whether there are good ETs or bad ETs, ETs who want the best for Earth and humanity, ETs who want to harm us, or ETs who don't really care about us either way, we'll never really know until they decide to come out of the galactic closet and fess up. In the meantime, we can set a good example for them by being kind to each other, respecting each other and doing our best for all life on Earth.

"Even if the aliens are short, dour, and sexually obsessed - if they're here, I want to know about them."

Carl Sagan

33

Q: What do we think and feel about ETs?

A 2015 poll[65] showed that the majorities of the public in Britain, Germany and the United States believe that living creatures with the ability to communicate and who do not come from Earth exist. In other words, most people who participated in the poll believe that ETs are real. Unfortunately, the poll didn't reveal how its respondents thought and felt about the purported ETs. As an experiencer therapist, I work with people who usually have very strong feelings about ETs and, consequently, I am interested in the thoughts and emotions that human beings experience as a result of ET contact.

During my many years of studying human-ET contact and working with individuals who are involved in this phenomenon up-close and personally, I have come across varied and unexpected answers when questioning experiencers about what they think and feel about ETs. That's not surprising, however, considering that humans rarely share the same feelings and opinions about anything, and especially things as controversial as contact with alien beings.

However, in the past few years, a handful of formal studies have reached out to experiencers and begun shedding light on the physiological, psychological and emotional effects of contact, and as the emphasis in Ufology expands outward from the nuts-and-bolts paradigm into the realms of intelligence and consciousness, I suspect that we will continue to find more insightful and surprising answers. More than that, however, it's my belief that the ramifications of this question will extend beyond the intellectual and emotional experiences of individual contactees to actually shape the future of humanity.

Why does it matter?

Why does it matter what humans think and feel about ETs? Most people would say it doesn't, but they would be wrong. Like everything else we experience in life, our contact with alien beings has an effect

---

[65] *You are not alone: most people believe that aliens exist.* YouGov.com. Sept. 13-14, 2015.

on us. No one comes away from an interaction with extraterrestrials unchanged - for good or ill. And what we think and feel about those interactions and the beings involved in them is vitally important, because it reflects how those interactions are changing us, first, as individuals, and then as time goes on, as societies, and eventually, as a species. Change is inevitable. As long as we have organic physical bodies subject to time and the environment, we can't avoid it, and if ETs are really here, then what we think and feel about them is a window to understanding how their presence is changing us, as individuals and humanity as a whole.

Generally and historically

It's not surprising that most experiencers who have had positive contact think of ETs as enlightened, beneficent beings, worthy of our confidence and trust. Likewise, individuals with less than positive contact experiences tend to think and feel the opposite - that alien beings don't respect or care about humanity and should not be trusted. Some experiencers relate that when they were first taken, the contact they experienced was terrifying, but as time passed and contact continued, it became more positive and they felt less fearful and more trusting. Interestingly, current research indicates that the majority of individuals who have ET contact view their experiences as positive, with those who view their experiences as negative in the minority.

Generally, if you look at ET contact events throughout history, earlier contact reports tended toward the negative, threatening variety, and while there are still negative contact reports, those now seem to be outweighed by the positive variety. Obviously, something has changed, but what? Did our alien visitors get more sensitive and compassionate or did we get more courageous and tolerant? We know that human beings are highly adaptable and capable of changing our thoughts, feelings and attitudes with relative ease. Are ETs capable of doing the same? Has some kind of mutual understanding developed between humans and ETs as intellectually equal, conscious beings? Or, as some people think, is it all just a deceit on the part of the aliens to lull us into trusting them and letting down our guard?

What are we supposed to think about ETs?

Unless they are involved in the UFO/ET field, most people don't spend time talking or thinking about ETs, and those of us who do, if we are honest, must admit that we still have a long way to go to reach a full understanding of them and the contact phenomenon as a whole.

And yet, while no one has deciphered the entire UFO/ET enigma, there is no shortage of individuals and groups who presume to tell the rest of us what we are supposed to think and feel about ETs, and some of them are pretty hard to ignore because they are the individuals and institutions we have learned to respect and trust throughout our lives. So, what are they telling us to think about ETs?

• *Medicine/Psychology* - ET contact is not real. All abduction/contact events are actually hallucinations, sleep paralysis, dreams, psychotic events or drug or alcohol-induced aberrations or fantasies. If you believe you have been in contact with ETs, you are deluded or ill and you need medical help.

• *Science* - ETs may exist, but if they do, they don't interact with humans. The distances are too great to make interplanetary or interstellar travel practical, and ETs wouldn't come to Earth anyway, because humanity is too technologically backward to make such an effort worthwhile. And if they did come, it would only be to conquer or destroy us. If you think you have been in contact with ETs, you are misguided. If you're a scientist and think you have been in contact with ETs and you value your career, keep it to yourself.

• *Religion* - Some religious groups tell us that ETs don't exist. Some say they do exist, but they are evil and should be avoided. Some more open-minded religions allow that ETs exist and are part of God's creation, but it's the church's job to reach out and show them the path to salvation, so we should leave it to them. In general, it's okay to think that ETs may be "out there somewhere," but if you think you've been in contact with them, you should confess, pray for forgiveness and try to forget the whole thing.

Other points of view

Being taken by alien beings against one's will would be horrifying and abhorrent to most of us, but some experiencers say they actually enjoy it. Most individuals who feel this way aren't mentally ill nor are they masochists who enjoy inflicting pain on themselves. But they do relish the excitement and exhilaration of exploring the unknown, and they are willing and able to tolerate the possible unpleasant aspects of contact in exchange for the opportunity of experiencing what few other humans ever will.

Some individuals who have successfully resisted contact say, for the most part, they enjoyed the experiences and the only reason they ended them was because they never knew in advance when they were going to be taken or they didn't want their children taken. Other experiencers say their contact with ETs is spiritually uplifting and consciousness-expanding and they are grateful for the privilege of being chosen. And yet other experiencers tell of developing deep emotional attachments and even romantic and sexual relationships with ETs that have lasted years.

Many experiencers say they don't like every aspect of contact, but they respect the ETs they interact with and feel that they are respected in return. Many actually look forward to upcoming contact events and are disappointed when there are none for long periods of time or if contact stops altogether. One experiencer said his experiences are always a bit frightening and emotionally difficult, but when the ETs don't come for a long time, he misses them and wants to see them again.

We often see love-hate scenarios in human relationships, and it appears to be the same in some human-ET relationships. It may not make sense, but many aspects of the human personality don't make sense, and yet they are undeniable parts of ourselves, and some of the ETs who interact with humans on Earth appear capable of touching those parts.

Star families

Based on the conversations I have had with several hybrid individuals, it seems that while the ET branch of their family may not be perfect, it's usually less difficult to deal with than the human branch. Of course, that's understandable, since it's the human branch that they usually face the everyday vicissitudes of life on Earth with. But despite the problems, they all say the joy and personal rewards that come from their human life, including the love and respect they feel for their Earth families, is worth any difficulties that come with it. At the same time, I have never spoken with a human-alien hybrid who didn't feel love and respect for their ET family or group as well.

Q: What do we think and feel about ETs?

Does advanced technology = advanced wisdom?

The one thing everyone involved in Ufology agrees on is that the alien beings we have met are technologically superior to the past and present day iteration of Earth humans. This is obvious from the earliest sightings, reports and depictions of ET craft and contact experiences which, although they may vary in many respects, seldom vary in descriptions of the level of technology present. No question about that. But does their technological superiority also mean that ETs are superior to us in every other way? Does hi-tech mean smarter, stronger and wiser? Early humans thought so and worshipped alien beings as all-powerful, all-knowing gods. Today we don't think of them as gods, but do we still think of them as all-knowing and ourselves as inferior?

Throughout the history of our world, we have seen that advanced technology doesn't always equal advanced wisdom, and as we move forward to closer contact with beings from other worlds, let us not forget that. Yes, we can learn a lot from our ET visitors, but they can also learn a lot from us - as our equals, not our superiors.

"In our time, the search for extraterrestrial life will eventually change our laws, our religions, our philosophies, our arts, our recreations, as well as our societies. Space, the mirror, waits for life to come look for itself there."

Ray Bradbury

Epilogue

Advice from Experiencers

Most of the experiencers I have worked with over the years are normal people living normal lives, apart from their ET contact experiences. Some of their contacts have been positive and some have been negative, and they have chosen to deal with the aftermath of those experiences in different ways. But by and large, they are caring, compassionate people who love life and want to help other people when they can. Many of them have plucked up the courage to ask the forbidden questions and have felt the sting of put-downs and condemnation as a result.

While they may be disappointed by the lack of interest that most UFO investigative organizations have shown in human-ET contact to date, many experiencers realize the importance of continuing study in the field, and are involved as researchers and investigators. Above all, they see it as their duty to help new experiencers and the general public alike to understand what human-ET contact is all about.

I learned long ago that if we want to understand human-ET relations, we must go to the source - the people who are involved up-close and personally in extraterrestrial contact - the individuals who have experienced the best and the worst and come through it all. They have wisdom, humor and great advice to share with anyone who thinks they might be an experiencer or anyone who is merely interested in the inside story of human-ET contact.

Here is their sage advice.

"I have had a variety of experiences with sightings, abductions and visitations, which I continue to experience to this day. If there is one thing I can share about my experiences it is this: the biggest thing I run into with people if they're not simply disbelieving me about it is their questions about whether or not aliens are going to conquer earth, eat us, turn us into slaves, or exploit earth's natural resources. This is psychological projection. We do these things. We've been doing these things to less

203

technologically advanced societies and our own countries for a long time. For example, the conquering of the Native Americans and consequent destruction of their cultures by the white man, hundreds of years of slavery, the Holocaust, sex trafficking. Every country has their version of it. We're projecting the things we do onto other cultures beyond this planet, assuming that they'll treat us like we've been treating each other over millennia. Nothing could be further from the truth. Believe it or not, they are fascinated by us because we have one quality that makes us singularly unique in the universe and that one quality tragically is what we try to divest ourselves of. It is our ability to imagine things - our creativity. When I ask them why they come here, that is what they say. My advice to anyone wanting to understand experiences they may have had or hope for if they haven't had any is to be open about what it could mean. And make sure you're not projecting your own fear onto something that doesn't need to be feared." PS

"Have you got three hours? Just kidding. There's so much I could say, but I'll try to keep it short. I've been up and down with ETs for a long time now and the best advice I can give new experiencers is that in the long run it doesn't matter what ETs do to you or what so-called experts write or say about it, what matters is what you choose to make of it. You're in charge of your life. I don't know anybody who grew up in a rose garden - we all have problems and nobody has a perfect life. Even not-perfect lives have good times so try to focus on those. And another thing, you're not crazy - unless you are. I mean, if you have mental illness there'll be other signs and you should get help ASAP, but just because you've been with ETs doesn't mean you're nuts. There's a lot of crap out there about this subject and not everyone who talks about it knows what they're talking about so don't take everything you hear or read in books or the internet as gospel truth. If you see or hear something that's scary or offensive to you, put it down or turn it off cause that kinda stuff isn't helpful. Try to keep your sense of humor and get out and do something

for someone else, get involved, do fun stuff that gets your mind focused on other things. This is your show. You can do it. I did." MH

"I have been an experiencer since I was 2 years old, I will be 74 his year. I have known love, caring, appreciation, healings, as well as protection. I have been wounded, suffered torturous procedures on surgical tables but always with reassurance that it will not kill me. If I were to give any advice it would be not to be afraid. This has been going on long before you. You were not afraid before you knew about it, so nothing has changed, except now you know." PD

"Are you sure you wanna hear this? Okay, what really burns my butt is people who stand up on the stage in UFO conferences and write books claiming to know all about UFOs, ETs and contact, when they've never actually been on board a UFO, seen an ET or been in contact with them. I'm not gonna say that contact is always pleasant and I think people do need to know what's going down and the truth should be told, but not when people act like they know the truth when they don't. Even researchers and investigators who have interviewed lots of abductees still don't get it right when they say they know the truth. Until you have talked to every single one of us you won't know the truth - the story's just too big and everyone who has been there has a piece of it but not the whole thing. What I would say to other abductees if you are having trouble because of contact, don't try to deal with it on your own. If you're okay, then it's no biggie, but if you're not, get help. And I wish you the best!" AW

"I gave up trying to talk to anyone about my ET stuff a long time ago because when I was growing up I didn't like being laughed at and now as an adult with a career in the sciences I don't want to lose my job or be thought of as an idiot. I believe we're never going to see the big picture of what's going on in the universe if we just keep looking through the perspective of science and technology. That might work with robots or AI, but not with humans. I

think the new work that is being done in consciousness is the next step that we should be pursuing. We need to keep at it because as time goes on more and more people will be open and upcoming generations will follow our lead and eventually find the truth. To my fellow scientists and debunkers I would say that you are fighting a losing battle, the human mind and spirit is limitless and won't be held back by your blindness. Thanks for the chance to say this." TR

"What I have learned about the ET-human connection, from my experience, took me totally by surprise. I had a lifetime of visits by ETs that started in my early childhood, conscious visits that always terrified me. Then one day, I realized these visitations had ceased. Amazed, I found myself sadden, heartbroken, rejected. How can they just dump me like this? Apparently there was more to this story than I could consciously remember — a relationship had taken place. One that meant something to me deeply and I didn't really want it to stop. So after awhile I got over it and moved on. My job for them was done. So if you're having visits by ETs, maybe it's not so bad after all. Yes. One other thing I would suggest if possible, tell your story. Something I failed to do with my family. I discovered an interesting thing about one of my parents that I wished I had known earlier. If I would have talked to them about it, it might have explained some of this. Now I will never get the chance. They have all passed away." KW

Great advice! Thanks Everyone!

APPENDIX

Signs that you may be a starseed

1. You didn't fit in as a child and felt different from other kids. You may have been advanced in some way like talking, walking or reading much earlier than your peers.

2. You have a strong feeling of wanting to "go home" and a feeling of what this home is like, even if you can't put it into words.

3. You had strong psychic and paranormal experiences as a child which continue into the present. Seeing spirits, seeing into the future or beyond the lines of time, having prophetic dreams, seeing a UFO or having an alien encounter are all somewhat normal experiences for starseeds.

4. You are highly sensitive to light, sound and energy in your environment.

5. You are strongly empathic and can feel the emotions of others and possibly hear their thoughts, which allows you to easily read people.

6. Communication with other people may seem slow and sometimes painful for you when you already know what the other person is going to say, sometimes before they do.

7. You have deep inner wisdom and you feel timeless.

8. You may have had dreams or memories of off-planet past lives and experiences in totally different dimensions and ways of existing.

9. You have a strong sense of your personal mission, even if you don't know what it is yet. You have the burning desire or feeling that you are meant to do something big.

10. You have intense and vivid dreams that often happen in places and times which are off-planet. Some of these dreams are so vivid they seem more real than reality.

11. Small children and babies seem fascinated by you - like they are able to see your uniqueness and your bright light.

12. You have a deep connection with nature, plants, animals and the physical elements, and you seem able to communicate with them on a certain level.

13. You don't fit in with society. Others consider you to be strange or weird and may be somewhat wary of you.

14. You often feel as if you are "on the outside looking in" at the rest of the world.

15. You may not have many friends, and those who you do connect with seem to have a deep and complex relationship with you which spans time and space.

16. You may feel alienated by your parents and immediate family like they don't "get you" and you don't "get them." You may have even wondered at times if you were adopted.

17. You are very aware of energy and how the energy of others can affect you. You may have created energetic protection techniques to be able to handle being around others, and large crowds or busy places can energetically overwhelm you.

18. You have natural psychic gifts and channeling or energy healing abilities.

19. You know you are here from the stars to serve humanity and Earth in reaching the higher dimensions, and you are actively taking steps to remember more of your soul's truth and to accomplish your purpose as a star being.

20. You know that you are more than just a physical being and that your true essence is as a spiritual light being.

Adapted from asking.angels.com

Common characteristics of ET contact

The following list has been compiled by experiencer therapists and researchers, and represents the most commonly reported characteristics and signs of ET contact. It's important to remember that there can be explanations for most of them that have nothing to do with ET contact. However, if several of these apply to you, it's likely that you are an experiencer.

Missions or Goals

Do you have a strong feeling or compulsion that you have a mission or important task to perform without knowing where this compulsion comes from?

Do you secretly feel that you are special or were chosen to do something, but you may not know what that something is?

Do you have a cosmic awareness or a special interest in the environment or issues affecting the Earth?

Do you frequently think or dream about disasters or Earth changes such as earthquakes or floods, with a conviction that they are going to happen?

Sleep

Do you have trouble sleeping through the night for reasons that you can't explain?

Have you ever awakened during the night startled and feeling as though you have just dropped onto your bed from a height?

Do you feel that you need to sleep with your bed against a wall in order to feel safe or sleep in some other peculiar manner to be safe?

Do you ever hear popping or buzzing sounds or any other unusual sounds or physical sensations upon waking or going to sleep that you can't account for in your normal environment?

Have you seen a hooded figure or other beings next to your bed at night?

Have you ever experienced a sudden overwhelming desire to go to sleep when you had not planned to, and you weren't able to prevent yourself from doing so without having a physical condition such as narcolepsy?

Have you awakened in the morning or the middle of the night to find yourself in a different location in your home (or outside your home) or a different position in your bed, or wearing different clothing from when you went to sleep, or with your clothing damaged?

Dreams & memories

Do you have dreams in which superior beings, angels or aliens are educating you about humanity, the universe, global changes or future events?

Do you have a conscious memory or a dream of being outside your body?

Do you dream about seeing UFOs or being inside a UFO and interacting with UFO occupants?

As a child or teenager was there a special place that you secretly believed had special meaning just for you?

Do you have dreams of being chased by animals or half animal/half other beings?

Do you have an obsessive memory or dream that will not go away, such as seeing an alien face or a strange baby, or an examination table or needles, etc.?

Have you had dreams of passing through a solid wall, closed window or door?

Have you had dreams of non-human doctors or strange medical procedures being performed on you?

Do you have conscious memories that you believe did not happen the way you recall them?

Unreasonable fears

Do you secretly fear being accosted or kidnapped if you do not constantly monitor your surroundings, with no grounds for doing so?

Have you frequently found yourself repeatedly checking through your home before you go to bed at night with no grounds for doing so?

Are you now or have you ever been afraid of your closet or what might come out of it?

Are you afraid of medical or dental examinations or treatment, or do you fear the same for your children?

Do you have an abnormal fear of the dark?

Do you feel like you are being watched frequently, especially at night?

Do you have very strong fears or phobias, such as an unreasonable fear of heights, insects, certain sounds, bright lights or being alone?

Do you have a fear of looking into the eyes of animals or do you dream of looking closely into the eyes of animals?

UFOs and ETs

Do you have a feeling that you are not supposed to talk about alien beings or about encounters with alien beings or UFOs?

Do you have a strong interest or obsession with the subject of UFO sightings or aliens or a compulsion to read about the subject, or do you have a strong aversion towards the subject?

Have you ever seen a UFO in the sky or close to you within a short walking or driving distance?

If you have seen a UFO, were you compelled to follow it? If you did, did you feel that its occupants were aware of you?

Have you had someone in your life who claims to have witnessed a UFO or alien being near you?

Have you had someone in your life who claims to have witnessed you being missing for a period of time with no explanation?

Unexplained things happening around you

Did you experience a period of time while you were awake that you don't remember, and you don't remember what you did during that time?

Do you sometimes hear a high-pitched noise in one or both of your ears that you can't attribute to tinnitus or anything else?

Have you seen someone near you become motionless or physically frozen in time, especially someone with whom you were sleeping?

Do you recall having a secret playmate or secret playmates when you were a child?

Have you noticed electronic devices around you go haywire or malfunction without explanation, such as streetlights as you walk under them or TVs or radios as you move near them or cars you were in?

Do you frequently see combinations of multiple digits, such as 111 or 444, or other repeating patterns on clocks, digital displays or in any other setting?

Have you seen balls of light, orbs or flashes of light in your home or other locations?

Have you seen a strange fog or haze that was not due to weather and should not be there?

Have you heard strange humming or pulsing sounds around you for which you could not identify the source?

Health or physical issues with no standard medical diagnosis or common explanation

Have you had nosebleeds or found blood stains on your pillow when you awakened in the morning for unexplained reasons?

Do you frequently have sinus problems or migraine or cluster headaches?

Have X-rays or other procedures revealed foreign objects lodged in your body that cannot be explained?

Have you been medically diagnosed with the following: chronic fatigue syndrome, brain sleep disturbance, Gulf War Syndrome, fibromyalgia, myofascial pain, Epstein-Barr or other immune disorders?

For women only: have you had a false pregnancy or a verified pregnancy that disappeared within two or three months, frequent female problems or reproductive difficulties?

Have you had sore muscles upon waking up without exercise or strain before going to sleep?

Have you felt paralyzed in your bed or at home for no apparent reason without being medically diagnosed with chronic sleep paralysis?

Have you found unusual scars, marks or bruises on your body with no possible explanation as to how you received them, especially small scoop-shaped indentations, straight-line scars, patterns of pin-prick marks, scars in the roof of your mouth, in your nose or behind one ear, triangular bruises or finger-tip sized bruises on the inside of your thighs or your arms?

Have you had frequent, recurring urinary tract infections that did not respond to medical treatment?

Has your drug or alcohol use suddenly changed significantly one way or the other?

Do you have an unusual fear of doctors, hospitals or needles or do you tend to avoid medical treatment?

Do you have frequent or sporadic headaches, especially in the sinus area, behind one eye or in one ear?

Symptomatology of PTSD relating to ET contact experiencers

Post-traumatic stress disorder (PTSD) is a type of anxiety disorder triggered by either witnessing or experiencing a traumatic event, especially when the event is outside the realm of an individual's typical experience. Encounters with alien beings are certainly outside most peoples' normal experiences, and even the most benign ET encounter can cause shock and trauma. And the traumatic event may not end when the event ends, but may be re-experienced in intrusive, recurring thoughts or distressing dreams for years after.

Many experiencers report flashbacks, low self-esteem and insomnia, and some have recurring dreams about trying to save themselves, their children or pets from being abducted. In addition, in PTSD, memories of the traumatic event may persist, causing an individual to avoid things associated with it. He may drive miles out of his way to avoid certain neighborhoods or stretches of road, or avoid getting needed medical or dental care due to a fear of examinations. He may even avoid taking his children to the doctor for the same reason.

An individual suffering from PTSD may experience persistent symptoms of increased arousal, such as staying awake at night or difficulty concentrating during the day. Experiencers may wake up at the same time night after night for no known reason, or purposely stay awake at night hoping to avoid being abducted.

Treatment for PTSD typically consists of some type of cognitive behavior therapy designed to change disturbing thought patterns, improve symptoms, teach skills to deal with issues and help restore self-esteem. Hypnotherapy may also be used. Depending on the individual, family or group therapy may be a good choice rather than private therapy.

Most contactee/abductees have some temporary difficulties adjusting and coping, but they don't suffer from symptoms that require medical treatment. However, if the difficulties get worse and interfere with a person's day-to-day functioning for longer than a month, he or she should seek help from a qualified medical professional.

Are you a military abductee (milab)?

If you are an ET experiencer or abductee, there is a possibility that your contacts may be milabs - abductions by humans disguised as ETs that are sponsored by agents of human governments or militaries - or they may be genuine ET contact with milab involvement. Milabs are not as common as other types of contact, but if you suspect that it's true for you, the following list can serve as a guide to help you determine what's going on. But keep in mind that nothing on the list can determine, for certain, if that is what you are dealing with.

1. Have you been abducted by human military personnel without aliens being present?

2. Have you seen aliens and military personnel together in the same environment? Was it on an alien ship or other alien environment or base?

3. Do you or members of your family have a connection to any military, NASA or aerospace industry, or hold a high-level security clearance?

4. Do you currently, or have you ever, lived near a military base?

5. Did alien beings instruct you in any of their technology? Have you flown, navigated or worked the controls on an alien ship?

6. After being abducted by alien beings, have you experienced harassment by any of these: black helicopters, telephone interruption/noise, calls at all hours of the day and night, mail or email tampered with or missing, being followed, being approached or confronted by military personnel or men-in-black?

7. Do you feel you have been remotely influenced by thoughts that are not your own to cause harm to yourself or others, and are you confident that you are not suffering from mental illness?

8. Have you ever felt like someone else was scanning the inside of your head, seeing through your eyes, involuntarily moving your body, or do you feel like your body is running energy that is not being generated naturally by your body?

9. Do you have alien abduction memories of being interrogated, intimidated, beaten or roughed-up by humans? Did you receive verbal warnings or threats to you or your family's safety?

10. Do you have psychic abilities? Do you astral travel (OBE), remote view, perform psychokinetics (move matter with your mind), or do telepathy (mind-to-mind communication) or mind reading?

11. During alien abductions, have you experienced human doctors performing medical procedures on you?

12. Have you ever seen back-engineered military vehicles or aircraft? Have you traveled in any?

13. Have you ever seen any of the following during an abduction: elevators, long gray hallways, partitioned rooms, tents, clean rooms, haz-mat type tented environments, bright fluorescent lights or other lighting fixtures?

14. Were you ever in the Gifted Student Program, MENSA, had exceptional SAT scores or were you recognized for having genius or very high intelligence or creativity, scientific or physical talents or abilities?

15. Have you experienced long periods of missing time, such as days, weeks or months?

16. Do you recall, as a child, participating in a special "school" that your parents took you to, but that friends and maybe even your siblings were not involved in?

17. Do you suspect that you have a handler or a "teacher" who controls what you are allowed to do and feel?

Adapted from starseedawakening.org

The most commonly reported alien beings interacting with humans on Earth

Several types of extraterrestrial beings are purportedly in contact with humans on Earth, and their appearance, characteristics and methods of contact and communication vary widely. Experiencers and researchers estimate that the number of different alien races and groups range from 87 to over 200. The following are brief descriptions of some of the most commonly encountered and most often reported types.

Adromedans - From the Andromeda Constellation, these frequently channeled beings are similar to Earth humans, but are described with appearances ranging from blue skin to Nordic-type features (blonde hair/blue eyes/pale skin), Mediterranean-type features (light to dark brown hair/gray to brown eyes/tan skin), or Asian-type features (dark hair, dark slanted eyes and skin color that varies from pale to light tan/brown), and with or without wings. They are reportedly the oldest race in our galaxy, peaceful and scientific, and are very concerned with the welfare of humanity and the Earth.

Alpha Centaurians - From the Alpha Centauri system, the closest star and planetary system to the Earth. They are a humanoid species with aquatic features - gills and webbed feet and hands - that allow them to live in Earth's oceans. They are described as luminous gray in color and of different heights. Supposedly in possession of highly advanced weapons systems, they claim that they are on a peaceful mission to assist Earth and humanity in its advancement and enlightenment. People frequently report past-life connections with these beings.

Altairans - These reptilians, or humanoid reptilians, are reported to be from the Constellation Aquila in the Altair system and are known as nomads of the stars, but they are also known to sometimes ally themselves with other groups such as the Ashtar Command, the Nordics, the Grays and reportedly even some Earth governments, for a variety of purposes. They are sometimes mistaken for other types of reptilians, who they resemble in some ways, but they claim that they don't participate in experiments on humans or organize human-alien hybridization programs.

Antarians - These humanoid beings are described as having light-colored hair and pale bluish skin, with red or blue eyes, and may be associated with underground bases, including bases under the Antarctic continent. It has been said that the light colored groups may be a pure Aryan race that was connected with Nazi experiments and developments during World War II. It has also been reported that there is a reptilian form of this species with pale yellow or bright green eyes and slitted pupils.

Apunians - These beings first made contact with humans in Peru in 1960. Humanoid, with dark skin and long, dark hair, they stand over seven feet tall, and are said to come from a more evolved galaxy which they originally referred to as X-9, but in later contacts they said was Alpha Centauri. They are contacted physically and/or holographically through artificially generated, visible space-time energy bubbles known as xendras, and making contact with them normally requires special physical, mental and spiritual preparation, because they maintain an energy state that is higher than humans. They state that their mission is "to help our terrestrial brothers . . . everything for others."

Arcturians - According to Edgar Cayce, these very ancient beings are the most advanced in our Galaxy, and they possess the ability of interplanetary and interdimensional travel. Despite their name, they probably don't originate from Arcturus, but from somewhere else in the constellation Bootes, where Arcturus is located.

Members of this race are usually described as having greenish-blue skin and large oval eyes. Their life purpose is their own spiritual development, and they are in contact with humans to assist us in that task as well. Many humans report being related to this race.

Blues/Greens - These beings have been described by those who've seen them as short and stocky, with wide faces that are dark blue or green in color and sometimes have a comic appearance. They are usually wearing a uniform of some type, appear to float or glide along, and most often are reported appearing with other beings, as their helpers.

Grays (Greys) - Reportedly, there are several different types of Grays. They are the most well-known of alien types, generally described as thin with oversized heads, standing 3½ to 6 feet tall and weighing anywhere from 50 to 90 pounds, with pale gray skin that has a texture similar to that of a dolphin or a whale. They are generally believed to be clones, unable to reproduce biologically. They don't have ears or discernible mouths, and appear to communicate through mental telepathy, but they do have large, black un-lidded eyes. The shorter variety are believed to be workers and may be androids in service to the taller, more intelligent members of the species. Grays are usually associated with human abduction and human-alien hybridization programs.

Neonates (Zetas or Zeta Reticuli Grays) - They physically resemble the rest of their species in height and build except their skin color can vary from gray to tan, their eyes have pupils and their faces have distinguishable features. In addition, they have five digits on each hand rather than four. This is reportedly the species involved in one of the 1947 alien crashes near Roswell, New Mexico.

Insectoids - These insect-like beings, with large eyes and thin bodies, typically resemble a praying mantis. Usually described as 4 to 7 feet tall, they are often accompanied by small grays, and are sometimes seen wearing hooded capes or robes. They are often reported serving as teachers or nannies with children during learning procedures aboard alien ships and as healers and guides with adult abductees. However, they have also been reported in connection with malevolent agendas.

Nordics (Agarthans, Orions and Pleiadeans/ Plejarans) - With their blonde to reddish-colored hair, blue or green eyes and pale-colored skin, Nordics are very human in appearance. They seem to be concerned with the spiritual evolution of humanity, and often remind contactees that we are closely related to them, although humans are at a lesser developmental stage. Many humans report having contact with and being related to these beings, and channel information from them.

Reptilians - Many experiencers report contact with different kinds of reptilian-type beings, who have agendas that vary from positive to negative and malevolent. Most experiencers who have had contact with this type of alien describe them as non-humanoid, but with the ability to stand and walk upright, having typical reptilian features such as slitted eye pupils, dark gray-green scaly flesh, and nails that resemble talons. Some have tails and some no tails, they come in a variety of heights and some have wings. There is also at least one species of aquatic reptilian that reportedly is in contact with humans.

Draconians (Dracos or Dracs) are the most commonly seen and reported species of reptilian alien. They are large, intelligent and cunning, with the ability to shapeshift and mask as humans. Reportedly, they live in caverns underneath the surface of the Earth, where they have been for thousands of years, and they have the capacity for interdimensional travel. Encounters with them are nearly always reported as negative.

Sirians - The Sirian system consists of two, or possibly three, stars and is the home of many galactic species, both physical and non-physical, humanoid and non-humanoid. They have been part of mankind's history since the beginning and are known as devoted to mankind. Most of these races are quite benevolent, but there is a minority of negative species which are reportedly responsible for some of the more horrific human abductions. The Sirian race stems from Vega, and those from Sirius A were originally dark-skinned with dark, pronounced eyes, but the Sirians who stayed on Earth had a lot of contact with the lighter-skinner Lyrans and over time adapted to the climatological conditions on Earth, so their skin became lighter in color. Those who come from Sirius B are red, beige, gray or black-skinned in appearance, as well as reptilian and aquatic beings, such as dolphins and whales on Earth.

Venusians - This group of humanoid aliens supposedly hails from the planet Venus in our solar system, where they inhabit subterranean installations. Their physical appearances differ in height, weight, eye, hair and skin colors, and they can blend into everyday human society easily. Reportedly, they are in contact with humanity to guide and teach us how to raise our consciousness, and have also been in contact with the United States government, and maybe other world governments, in the past.

Iargans- a race of intelligent beings from the planet Iarga, approximately ten light years distant from our Sun. They are humanoid, similar to us physically, but with a heavier build, webbed feet, and heads and faces that have a canine appearance. They believe they are the ancestors of human beings, and their home planet has a social structure similar to ours, but without war, disease or deprivations like we have. They observe human activities from their oceangoing scout craft, but their spaceships never land on Earth. They don't abduct humans, but do occasionally invite individuals to visit their underwater craft and learn about them.

On-line Resources

Experiencer Therapy

Michelle Emerson
michelleconsults@gmail.com

Barbara Lamb
barbara.lamb.therapist@gmail.com

Hypnosis & Spirit Releasement

Linda Bennet, Ph.D.
lbennett@lindahypnoqueen.com

Contact Seminars / Retreats

Lyssa Royal Holt
https://www.lyssaroyal.net/lyssa-royal-holt.html

Research & Investigations

Kathleen Marden
https://www.Kathleen-marden.com

Journal of Abduction Research (JAR)
https://www.facebook.com/realjarmag

The Edgar Mitchell Foundation for Research into Extraterrestrial
and Extraordinary Encounters (FREE)
https://www.experiencer.org

The Mutual UFO Network (MUFON)
https://www.mufon.com

Paranormal Counseling

Denise Stoner
dstoner1@gmail.com

Websites

Rebecca Hardcastle Wright, PhD
https://www.exoconsciousness.com

Mutual UFO Network (MUFON)
https://www.mufon.com

The Center for the Study of Extraterrestrial Intelligence (CSETI)
https://www.cseti.org

The Organization for Paranormal Understanding and Support
(OPUS) https://www.opusnetwork.org/

The Alien Jigsaw
https://www.alienjigsaw.com

The Watcher Files
Known Types of Aliens and Races
https://www.thewatcherfiles.com/alien races.html

Matrix World Disclosure
ET Races Who Contact the Earth
https://www.matrixdisclosure.com/ets-extraterrestrial-races/

Thought Screen Helmet
https://www. stopabductions.com

Bibliography

Beyond UFOs: The Science of Consciousness and Contact with Non Human Intelligence - Volume 1, 2019. The Dr. Edgar Mitchell Foundation for Research into Extraterrestrial and Extraordinary Experiences (FREE). 2019.

Millennial Hospitality. Charles James Hall. Charles Hall. 2002.

Human by Day, Zeta by Night: A Dramatic Account of Greys Incarnating as Humans. Judy Carroll. Wild Flower Press. 2011.

X2: Healing, Entities and Aliens. Adrian Dvir. Adrian Dvir. 2000.

Beyond Strange: True Tales of Alien Encounters and Paranormal Mysteries. Bob and Trish MacGregor. Crossroads Press. 2017.

Journal of UFO Studies, by June O. Parnell, Ph.D. J. Allen Hynek Center for UFO Studies n.s. 2, 45-48. 1990.

Addendum to Conclusions on Nine Psychologicals, Final Report on the Psychological Test of UFO Abductees, by Elizabeth Slater, Ph.D. Fund for UFO Research. 1985.

UFO Evidence: A Scientific Study of the UFO Phenomenon and the Search for Extraterrestrial Life, by Caroline McLeod, et al. Psychological Inquiry, Vol. 7, No. 2. 1996.

Psychological characteristics of abductees: Results from the CUFOS abduction project, by M. Rodeghier, J. Goodpaster, S. Blatterbauer. JUFOS, Vol. 3. 1991.

Close Encounters: An example of UFO experiencers, by N.P. Spanos, P.A. Cross, K. Dickson and S.C. DuBreuil. Journal of Abnormal Psychology 102(4), 624-632. 1993.

Personality Characteristics on the MMPI, 16PF and ACL of Persons Who Claim UFO Experiences, by June O. Parnell, PhD. University of Wyoming. 1986.

Daimonic Reality: A Field Guide to the Otherworld. Patrick Harpur. Pine Winds Press. 1994.

UFO Healings: True Accounts of People Healed by Extraterrestrials. Preston E. Dennett. Wild Flower Press. 1996.

Close Extraterrestrial Encounters: Positive Experiences with Mysterious Visitors. Richard J. Boylan and Lee K. Boylan. Wild Flower Press. 1994.

Healing From UFOs. Gordon Creighton. Flying Saucer Review, 15:21-22. 1999.

Preparing for Contact: A Metamorphosis of Consciousness. Lyssa Royal and Keith Priest. Royal Priest Research. 1994.

Meet the Hybrids: The Lives and Missions of ET Ambassadors on Earth. Barbara Lamb and Miguel Mendonça. Amazon CreateSpace. 2015.

Raechel's Eyes: The Strange But True Case of a Human-Alien Hybrid. Helen Littrell and Jean Bilodeaux. Wild Flower Press. 2005.

The fantasy prone personality: Implications for understanding imagery, hypnosis, and parapsychological phenomena. In Imagery: Current Theory, Research and Application, 340-390, by Sandra Wilson and Theodore X. Barber. A.A. Sheikh (editor). Wiley. 1983.

The Omega Project: Near Death Experiences, UFO Encounters and Mind at Large. Kenneth Ring. Morrow/Harper Collins. 1992.

The Marden-Stoner Study on Commonalities Among UFO Abduction Experiencers. Kathleen Marden and Denise Stoner. 2012.

Facing the Shadow, Embracing the Light: A Journey of Spiritual Renewal and Awakening. Niara Terela Isley. Niara Terela Isley. 2003.

How to Defend Yourself Against Alien Abduction. Ann Druffel. Three Rivers Press. 1990.

Mechanisms of Contact: Does UFO Intelligence "Hoax" Encounters for Experiencers? Joseph Burkes, M.D. 2015, edited 2018.

Fire in the Sky: The Walton Experience. Travis Walton. Marlow & Company. 1996.

Abduction: Human Encounters With Aliens. John E. Mack, M.D. Charles Scribner's Sons. 1994.

Apparitions. G.N.M. Tyrrell. Gerald Duckworth and Co. Ltd. 1943.

Secret Life: Firsthand, Documented Accounts of UFO Abductions. David Jacobs. Fireside. 1993.

Passport to the Cosmos. John E. Mack, M.D. White Crow Books. 1999.

Secret Vows: Our Lives With Extraterrestrials. Denise Rieb Twiggs and Bert Twiggs. Wild Flower Press. 1992.

Into the Fringe: A True Story of Alien Abduction. Karla Turner, Ph.D. Wordswithmeaning.org. 2914.

Undersea UFO Base: An In-Depth Investigation of USOs in the Santa Catalina Channel. Preston Dennett. Blue Giant Books. 2018.

UFO Contact from Planet Iarga: A Report of the Investigation. Stefan Denaerde and Wendelle Stevens. Wendelle C. Stevens. 1982.

USOs - Unidentified Submerged Objects. www.tarrdaniel.com/documents/Ufology/uso.html.

U.F.O.s - at 450 Fathoms! Ed Hyde. Man's Illustrated, March 1996.

Journeys Out of the Body. Robert A. Monroe. Doubleday. 1971. Reprint Broadway Books. 2001.

The exteriorization of the mental body: a scientific interpretation of the out-of-the-body experience known as pneumakinesis. James Baker, Jr. William-Frederick Press. 1954.

With the Eyes of the Mind: An Empirical Analysis of Out-of-Body States. Glen O. Gabbard and Stuart W. Twemlow. Praeger Publishers. 1984.

Beyond the Light Barrier: The Autobiography of Elizabeth Klarer. David Klarer. Light Technology Publishing. 2009.

10 People Who Claim To Have Sexual Encounters With Aliens. https://listverse.com.

Love and Saucers: The Far Out World of David Huggins. Brad Abraham, Matt Ralston and Grant Ibrahim. Curator Pictures & Perceive Think Act Films. 2017.

You are not alone: most people believe that aliens exist. YouGov.com. Sept. 13-14, 2015.

About the Author

Gwen Farrell is a Certified Hypnotherapist specializing in Experiencer Therapy, she is an experiencer support group facilitator, UFO Field Investigator consultant, CE-5 researcher, speaker and author.

Professional Affiliations

Academy of Clinical Close Encounter Therapists (ACCET) - Secretary/Treasurer.

Organization for Paranormal Understanding and Support (OPUS) - contributor.

Mutual UFO Network (MUFON) - member, field investigator, MUFON Journal contributing writer, consultant, Experiencer Research Team member.

The Edgar Mitchell Foundation for Research into Extraterrestrial and Extraordinary Encounters (FREE).

Journal of Abduction Research (JAR) - Board of Editors.

Contact

Gwen Farrell, CHt, RT
etherapist.gf@gmail.com

Other writing by
Gwen Farrell, CHt, RT

Forbidden Questions: A Therapist Talks About Human-ET Contact,
Trafford Publishing, 2017.

For The Mufon Journal

How Belief Systems Affect ET Contact Experiences

ET Contact and Phobias

Am I an ET Experiencer?

Should I Get Therapy for my ET Experiences?

For The Journal of Abduction Research (JAR)

Sleep Paralysis and Alien Abductions

Milabs – Military Abductions

Why Don't I Remember my ET Visits?

Do ETs Control the Narrative?

Can I Make Contact With ETs?

Natural Functions of the Mind Are Not Explanations for Alien Abductions

Experiencer Therapy is More Than Hypnosis

Birds of a Feather - Will Sharing my ET Experiences in a Group Help Me?

What About Implants?

For The Academy of Clinical Close Encounter Therapists (AC-CET)

ETs Heal Humans in Alternative Clinics

Brainwaves and ET Abductions

Articles for The Organization for Paranormal Understanding and Support (OPUS)

Can I Communicate With ETs?

Should I Get Therapy for My ET Contacts?

Why me?

Are All Contacts With ETs Like Mine?

Blog - http://etcontact-healing.blogspot.com

Made in the USA
Coppell, TX
12 June 2020